AMERICAN MOURNING

JOINED BY WAR—TORN BY BELIEFS

AMERICAN MOURNING

THE INTIMATE STORY OF TWO FAMILIES

CATHERINE MOY AND MELANIE MORGAN

WND BOOKS

AN IMPRINT OF CUMBERLAND HOUSE PUBLISHING, INC.

NASHVILLE, TENNESSEE

AMERICAN MOURNING

A WND BOOK

PUBLISHED BY CUMBERLAND HOUSE PUBLISHING, INC.

431 Harding Industrial Drive

Nashville, Tennessee 37211

Cover design by Duncan Design, Nashville, Tennessee

Library of Congress Cataloging-in-Publication Data

Moy, Catherine, 1961–
 American mourning : the intimate story of two families joined by war, torn by beliefs / Catherine Moy and Melanie Morgan.
 p. cm.
 Includes bibliographical references and index.
 ISBN-13: 978-1-58182-540-4 (hardcover : alk. paper)
 ISBN-10: 1-58182-540-4 (hardcover : alk. paper)
 1. Iraq War, 2003– 2. Iraq War, 2003– —Protest movements—United States. 3. Soldiers—Family relationships. 4. Mothers and sons. I. Morgan, Melanie, 1956– II. Title.
DS79.76.M675 2006
956.7044'3092273—dc22
[B]
 2006022659

Printed in the United States of America
1 2 3 4 5 6 7 8 9 10—10 09 08 07 06

To

JUSTIN JOHNSON,

CASEY SHEEHAN,

and the soldiers of the 1-82 Field Artillery Division

CONTENTS

FOREWORD

CATHERINE MOY AND MELANIE MORGAN have captured in this book an important part of the global war on terror and its impact on two American families: the Johnsons of Georgia and the Sheehans of California. These families represent all the American families who are carrying the burden of this war against Islamofascism, and they reflect dramatically different responses to their losses as a result of this struggle.

When I first read this book, it became very personal and compelling for me. I am a retired air force lieutenant general who served four combat tours in Vietnam. In that war, I lost my younger brother, Dick, as he was completing his second combat tour with the First Cavalry Division, the same division in which Casey Sheehan and Justin Johnson served in Iraq. On the very day Dick was killed, my older brother, Jim, had just entered the combat zone as commander of an F-105 squadron. (By the way, F-105 pilots had some of the highest losses in the air war over North Vietnam, which was not so encouraging to my family.) So my reading evoked eerie flashbacks of those days heavily laden with the concerned looks of parents, wives, children, aunts, uncles, cousins, and friends both in and out of the service. This was made especially poignant since Dick's widow and three very young children were living in Fairfield, California, which is close to Vacaville, where the Sheehans lived. These firsthand memories made this book so compelling to me that I could not put it down.

Casey Sheehan and Justin Johnson gave their lives for freedom and are good examples of why their generation will be

equated with the renowned greatest generation that fought and won World War II. Casey and Justin's battle is over, but our country's fight against Islamofascism is not yet over, nor, unfortunately, is the shared anguish of many more American families.

American Mourning is as much a story about the all-volunteer military and love for one's country as it is about the wonderful families that support our troops at home and overseas. Casey Sheehan and Justin Johnson grew up in different parts of America, but they bonded in the army's band of brothers as every soldier has in all previous wars. This bond can never be duplicated elsewhere, especially after it has been seared in the crucible of armed combat. It is why the Sheehan family could not understand Casey's reenlisting to go back to combat. It is why Justin enlisted after September 11, 2001, and why his brother, Joshua, also enlisted and why his father, Joe, went back in the army national guard and combat at the ripe old age of forty-five. The Johnsons are a magnificent symbol of America's inner strength, and wife and mother Jan Johnson, with all three of her men going into combat, was put through hell as few women have.

Patriotism and love of one's country seem to be passé to many liberals in America, but it is very obvious that America is still blessed with sons and daughters who possess this kind of love for their country and have the spirit to do something about it—even when one has parents who are as radical as Cindy Sheehan. What is so conflicting in America today is that so many profess not to know why we fight to keep this country free. Justin and Casey knew, and so do so many Gold Star mothers and fathers who have suffered the loss of their sons and daughters in this global war on terror. *American Mourning* describes many of these patriots by name and portrays their

wonderful efforts—through organizations like Move America Forward and Gold Star Mothers—to help Americans understand what's going on. Their courageous acts are so important to our winning this war. *American Mourning* helped me to get to know of the exploits of Melanie Morgan, Sal Russo, and Joe Wierzbicki, as well as Deborah Johns, Joseph Williams, Steve Hayes, and Gary Qualls, to name just a few parents of those wonderful heroes who have made the supreme sacrifice for the cause of liberty. Americans who have given their lives for our freedom are awe inspiring at the least. God bless them all.

What was even more important but not stated openly in these pages is the conviction of these parents and families regarding the nobility of their children's deaths. These Americans have resisted the misguided onslaught of the mainstream media because they know that it was not our own shortcomings but Islamic extremism that attacked us on 9/11. What muddies this conflict is that our enemy is not a country but an ideology. This creed was centered in Afghanistan at the time, but it now pervades the Middle East. This ideology of Islamofascism is as bad as fascism, Nazism, and Communism were in the twentieth century, and it must be defeated at its roots, just as we defeated these other ideologies in World War II, which resulted in the establishment of moderate governments in Italy, Germany, and Japan today.

What we are struggling with today is that we cannot defeat this ideology by only defending America at home. We must have a forward strategy so Islamofascism does not come here.

In the summer of 2005, Cindy Sheehan was touted by the media as a part of its misplaced strategy to stall and thwart George Bush's prosecution of this war on terrorism. There is no doubt about Cindy's love for her son Casey or her family

prior to Casey's tragic death, but her abandonment of her family, husband, and friends for her short-lived stardom is described fairly here. The authors are very careful to present facts and not spin.

At times like these, it it best to remember that some of the fiercest fighting of World War II—the Battle of the Bulge, Okinawa, Iwo Jima—occurred during the last six months of the war. Because the fighting in Iraq and Afghanistan has increased in intensity recently does not mean we are losing the current war. Our men and women are not dying in vain. On the contrary, history will show that they have delayed the spread of terror and they are winning the war on terror.

The Johnson and Sheehan families are not the same people they were when we first learned of them. In large part, who they were before they lost their precious sons has defined the roads they have since taken. One thing is certain, however: they will never again be as they were. There is a hole in their lives and in the nation's where boys named Casey and Justin once stood. And we can only hope and pray that someday, somehow the questions these two American families—and the families of all our men and women lost in war—ask themselves will be answered, and they will find the peace and understanding for which they yearn. God bless them all.

—*Thomas G. McInerney*

INTRODUCTION

J OE JOHNSON SLOGGED THROUGH open sewers in dirt roads and gagged at the stench that strangled Sadr City in Iraq. This was where his son had died, a roadside bomb ripping through his patrol truck and into his body. This was where Joe planned to retaliate, to avenge his son's death. He lived on hate; it fueled his every breath. The September 11, 2001, attack on America spurred Joe and his sons, Joshua and Justin, to join the service. So patriotism and anger already ran through Joe's veins before terrorists killed Justin.

"If somebody killed your son and you had a chance to kill that person, wouldn't you?" Joe answers whenever anyone asks why he chose to go to Iraq.

There is no crueler loss for a parent than the death of a child. At first the loss sears the soul with pain, then it numbs it. Reality isn't welcome when a parent mourns. During the war on terror that is burning brightly in Iraq and Afghanistan, parents and wives and brothers and sisters daily fear any visit by military officials. And they have come. More than twenty-five hundred times the women and men in dress uniform have relayed the words, "We regret to inform you . . ." Sometimes the words are dampened by their own tears.

Joe and Jan Johnson live in Georgia where men have learned how to use the tools of war for as long as the women have learned to brew sweet tea. Joe taught his sons, Joshua and Justin, what his daddy taught him: how to hold a rifle and a

shotgun and how to keep a bullet straight. It's important to be on the offense. Sometimes, though, the prey strikes back.

After Muslim terrorists attacked the United States on September 11, 2001, all three Johnson men signed up to serve in the armed forces. Justin was the first at the recruiters' office, then came Joshua, and then finally Joe. Joe was forty-five. He had already served in the navy and army, so the National Guard made him a soldier. Joe figured he was in pretty good shape for a forty-something, but he blew his knee out during a terrorist exercise while in training at Fort Lewis in Washington State.

Justin didn't have any problems with creaky knees while the army turned him into a soldier. When he went to Fort Hood in sweaty Texas, he met Casey Sheehan, a soldier from California who could fix anything that ails a vehicle. Casey and Justin hung out together and talked about the war and God and Justin's Honda. Both were quiet, strong, patriotic, and God-loving young men. Justin was a Protestant. Casey was Catholic. He had attended Catholic schools during elementary school and served as an altar boy all through high school.

Casey's mother, Cindy Sheehan, was shocked when her oldest son enlisted in the army and was even more surprised when he re-upped four years later with the United States at war with terrorists in Iraq and Afghanistan. Others knew he was a loyal soldier who loved his country. Cindy offered to take Casey to Canada so he would avoid service in Iraq. But Casey declined and went to war at the end of March 2004.

Pat and Cindy Sheehan visited Casey while he trained in the states and supported him, though they never backed the war in Iraq or President Bush. The last time Casey visited home was in December 2003. His friends said he seemed happy and pretty healthy, though he may have been nursing a cold. They said he

Joe was a Christian missionary who loved helping children. In Iraq, he was a different kind of missionary: one who dealt out payback with the best weapons Uncle Sam gave him. He chain-smoked Marlboros and sucked down strawberry Fanta soda whenever he could get one. His earlier training in the armed forces came back to him like riding a bike with flat tires. He was tough, but Iraqi children softened his heart. He liked giving the kids old watches and sunglasses.

What drove Joe to avenge his son's death? Was he fighting for Justin? Was this his own private war? Or did he serve as part of the U.S. Army's mission to protect the Iraqi people until they could protect themselves? Joe's story unfolds in these pages. We see a quiet man turn to lethal firepower in his quest to quell the eternal pain of mourning for his youngest son.

Joe executed his jihad as his wife tried to live in a some-times surreal world of grief. She tried to function with her husband in Iraq and her other son set to fight in Afghanistan. She sewed clothes for her granddaughter Justine and attended a support group for military families. Sometimes she was so bitter that she wanted to fight herself.

With the sensation welling around Cindy Sheehan as a grieving mother opposed to the war because of her son's death, the media began hounding the Johnsons after Justin's death because he was the first soldier from Floyd County to die in the Iraq War. But Jan told CNN and others that, even after her son's death, she supported the war as well as President Bush. The media dubbed her "the anti-Cindy Sheehan."

Every day that Joe fought in Iraq, Jan feared another visit from the people in full military dress and those fearful condolences.

While Joe fought the terrorists, Cindy railed against the

war. Casey's death on Palm Sunday 2004 ignited a transformation in her that took her from pain to anger and, finally, to a brand of martyrdom. Fans called her Mother Sheehan.

After their sons' deaths, Cindy Sheehan traveled the United States with her antiwar message and Joe sweated under fire in Iraq. Both were shooting at ghosts.

This is their story.

AMERICAN
MOURNING

HOLY WEEK

★ ★

Everyone assumed Casey was going to be a priest, because
he was so faithful to God and to the Church. He never
missed Mass even when he went into the army.
　　　　　　　　　　—*Cindy Sheehan*[1]

I tried to talk Justin out of getting such a dangerous job. I
guess he wanted to be like his old man and get an up-front
combat job.
　　　　　　　　　　—*Joe Johnson*

V ACAVILLE, CALIFORNIA, IS A town of some one hundred thou-
sand folks but still small enough that secrets last as long as
a cup of joe at the Perfect Blend Coffee House where locals
drink black coffee and play checkers. A twenty-four-hundred-
foot mountain range called Blue Ridge flanks one side of town,
and the northeastern tip of town spills into the Sacramento Val-
ley. Interstate 80 runs through it and leads to Sacramento if you
go thirty minutes northeast. San Francisco, known as "the city,"
is about an hour to the west.

Summer sets in Vacaville with a vengeance and dries her
acres of open grassland. When months go by without rain, a
north wind will raise the neck hair on veteran firefighters who
constantly battle roadside fires started by broken bits of Bud-
weiser bottles that magnify the sun. Every once in a while, a fire

runs with the wind and swallows thousands of acres, like in 1908 when Blue Ridge burned for two weeks straight, devouring acre after acre until it ate its way into Napa County. Fire season usually starts when the last of the spring rains are done with Vacaville. The hills' greenery gives way to waves of yellow straw, perfect fuel for a hungry fire.

Vacaville has four seasons, despite what Easterners believe. Summer can dance into the three digits on the thermometers that hang in old fruit-cutting sheds, and fall colors the fruit trees and vineyards that support Vacaville's historic agricultural personality. A fierce winter like the one Mother Nature unleashed on New Year's 2006 can be downright ugly. Hillsides suffered stretch marks as the earth slid down natural gulleys, creeks burst their banks, and hundred-year-old trees gave up their hold on life, tumbling onto roads, houses, trees, and, tragically, a man who wanted to look at the storm water frothing in Alamo Creek.

Storms and fire don't stop the people of Vacaville; their backs are strong from decades of farming and serving in the U.S. armed forces. Just outside of town is Travis Air Force Base, the largest wing in the Air Mobility Command, so Vacaville's residents are personally connected to the military. Their fathers, sisters, brothers, and neighbors have worked around the monster C-5 Galaxies that are the airlift muscle of the air force; they shop at the base exchange and visit their family doctors at David Grant Medical Center. Travis belongs inside the city limits of Fairfield, but Vacaville supports the military like a blood brother. Since World War II, the base has supported every U.S. conflict, stood against antiwar activists like Jane Fonda, brought home prisoners of war and the war dead, and hosted Air Force One. President George W. Bush stopped at Travis to

boost the morale of the base's troops after the attacks on September 11, 2001.

Travis is a key military component in the war on terror. Its planes transport equipment and troops to Iraq, Afghanistan, and anywhere warriors go. Three times a week, troops injured in Iraq have stopped for treatment at Travis's medical center ever since the United States fought back in Operation Iraqi Freedom.

The air force, government, and agriculture are Vacaville's skeleton, but private industries such as biotech are investing in Vacaville (which means "Cow Town" in Spanish). I-80 bisects the city and brings it diversity and crime from San Francisco, Berkeley, and other areas whose cultures were foreign to Vacaville before the migration.

For years, Vacaville was known for its most infamous resident, murderer and cult master Charles Manson, whom the state kept at the California Medical Facility. That changed in the summer of 2005, when Cindy Sheehan camped in a ditch a few miles from President Bush's Crawford, Texas, ranch.

PALM SUNDAY services at St. Mary's Church began at 7:30 in the morning on a classic spring day. Vacaville's temperature in the middle of summer can kill a camel, but April generally offers comfortable picnic and church weather. The hottest day Vacaville ever recorded on April 4 was back in 1960, when the temperature reached 87 degrees. On April 4, 2004, the temperature rose to a mild 66 degrees, pushed gently by a five-mile-an-hour wind that St. Mary's could detect as the back doors to the church opened for parishioners in their slacks and button-down oxford shirts. Ushers guided folks along the long aisle to their seats on either side of the church.

The church is a classic American Catholic design with the aisle ending at the altar and a life-size crucifix. A controversy over the crucifix roiled the parish for months. Half of the parishioners liked the "rising Christ" but others preferred the idea of a classic crucifix showing Jesus hanging by his arms as a symbol of the Lord's death and resurrection.

Politics took a break during Holy Week, when the parish prepared for the celebration of Palm Sunday, the day Jesus entered Jerusalem on a donkey to face his executioners on Good Friday. Palm Sunday is a holy day for Catholics, marking the beginning of the week when their Savior was crucified then rose from the dead three days later in fulfillment of the Scriptures. Priests hand out palms that are blessed with holy water. Some fold the palms into the shape of crosses; others hang them in their homes as a simple blessed leaf. The palm symbolizes Christ's freedom from his flesh. Thoughts of Jesus's suffering and death peak on Good Friday, the day of the Crucifixion, when Catholic churches cover their statues with black cloth to signify mourning.

Pat and Cindy Sheehan had attended church services at St. Mary's with their four children since they moved to Vacaville in 1993. Casey had served the church until he joined the army and left home seven years later. On his last day, he assisted the priests at Mass, and his family sat in the wooden pews and prayed. Cindy told friends she ached that her oldest child was leaving the nest of her home and St. Mary's Church. Before parishioners left Mass, Casey stood in front of the congregation to thank them for their support during his years in Vacaville. He said good-bye.

"And I'd like to ask everybody to pray for my mom," Casey said.

☆ ☆

ALL OF St. Mary's Palm Sunday Masses were finished when Cindy, Pat, and their children sat down for supper. They had the television tuned to Cable News Network (CNN) where the family saw burning Humvees, chaos, and death in Iraq.[2] Casey's unit was stationed in the area, but he was a mechanic, and it was unlikely that he would be caught in the firefight Cindy saw on television. The darkness of war, burning tires spewing black smoke, horrified the Sheehans.[3]

News reports stated that eight soldiers had been killed.

Cindy couldn't get the images out of her mind. Or the words: *Soldiers were killed.* Mothers can't halt incessant thoughts when their sons are in a war zone. They can't sleep, and the worry takes them to dark places. The endless news cycle spreads images and sounds around the world in seconds, so nervous mothers who can't sleep tune in and watch the war. Then their minds run from heaven to hell.

Eight soldiers. Burning Humvees.

Cindy couldn't easily sleep after Casey left for Iraq, so CNN and the Internet kept her company. She stayed up all night with her computer. She searched for news, anything to let her know where her oldest boy was fighting or sleeping or eating. It was as if she could follow Casey's footsteps as he marched toward war. She and Pat tried to stay close to their son. They were among the few families who visited the troops in Casey's unit while they were still stateside.

The burning Humvees and black skies haunted Cindy as she crept through the evening of Palm Sunday. They played like black-and-white silent movies. Smoke. Fire. Bullets. Bodies.

Her unease grew. Mothers who have lost a child will tell you

how premonitions haunt them. Sometimes it's just a vague feeling. For some, it's visceral. Some vomit. Some collapse. Some just wait by the phone to hear what they already know—their baby is dead.

Life should stop when your child is facing death, or when radicals in a faraway land have just slaughtered his buddies. It is cruel that way. Life murmurs along, laughing and crying and spinning.

The dogs needed exercise, and Cindy needed fresh air. The moon was almost full and gave enough light to paint shadows on the streets and sidewalks and to allow her to maneuver the obstacles she would encounter. Besides, Cindy and the dogs knew the sidewalks and driveways. She was comfortable in her neighborhood, a row of working-class homes with old cars in the driveways. But on this night, unease followed her.

The streets in this part of Vacaville are crowded with cars because there isn't enough room in the driveways. There is no such thing as a three-car garage in the area. Guys spend weekends working on their older-model cars. The Chevys, Fords, and stray Volkswagens sit on jacks in driveways waiting for somebody to tinker with them.

Cindy was on autopilot, her six-foot frame passing the quiet houses with calla lilies growing out front. Most of the yards lacked the fine grooming of upper-end homes where gardeners tend the greenery. But the lilies take little care and pop up every year around Easter, their graceful white flowers opening into the shape of a wine glass.

JAN JOHNSON watched CNN too and saw the balls of black smoke rolling out of Sadr City on Palm Sunday. She paced the

floors of her double-wide trailer, which sat in the middle of a three-hundred-acre mobile home park in Rome, Georgia. Her twenty-two-year-old son, Justin, was in Sadr City. At least that's what she thought. He was trained to roll with quick-response teams that rescue soldiers in the deadliest war zones.

The news showed a quick-response team working Sadr City.

"I couldn't keep my eyes off of CNN," Jan said.

She had grown up in a military town, and her husband had served in the navy and army. After September 11, 2001, her two boys and husband signed up to fight the terrorists who brought war to the United States. Her husband, Joe, told her not to watch the cable television networks that broadcast twenty-four hours of mayhem. "It will make you crazy," he told her. "And it ain't doin' nothin' to make us any safer." But Jan couldn't get away from the TV. The images of shot-up and burning American military trucks horrified and numbed her.

Justin was a gunner on a Humvee. He had two M249 light machine guns—called SAWS (squad automatic weapons)—so he could swing them 360 degrees and hit the terrorists at any angle. When he talked to his mom about the war, Justin was honest. He once told her that he worried some guys might buckle under fire. Soldiers sniff out the guys they know will keep their heads when bullets zing by them and roadside bombs rattle their vehicles.

Justin had a gun in his hand as soon as he learned to walk. He was a good shot, a sharp eye. But you don't know how you'll handle combat until the enemy engages you and your friends go down around you, and you don't know if you're going to die in the smoke and stink of fresh blood.

Jan figured the odds were against her son.

After watching hours of repeated war footage on twenty-four-hour news channels, sleep finally came to Jan. She tried fighting it so she could watch more on the war, look for signs of her son. She went to her bedroom in the front of the house and lay down by herself in the cold bed.

Joe was at Fort Lewis—near Tacoma, Washington—getting his body and mind in shape to fight in Iraq. He had been temporarily waylaid by a knee injury. Joe ached to be in Iraq, near Justin. He hoped the injury would heal quickly and not sideline him for too long. Their older son, Joshua, was preparing to go to Afghanistan, where Americans and coalition troops still battled the enemies of freedom. And Justin—maybe he was in the middle of the ambush and firefight she had just seen on TV.

☆ ☆

As CINDY and the dogs approached her house on their return from the evening walk, the sight of a military car rattled her. Ever since Casey had deployed to Iraq, she couldn't control the fear that taunted her nerves. Now soldiers waited at her house.

Maybe Casey is just wounded, she thought. *Maybe he's already home.*

Cindy's husband, Pat, was folding the laundry inside the house. It was around 9:00 p.m. when he heard a knock on the door. Cindy didn't usually knock.

When he opened the door, a horror movie began to play out inside the Sheehan home. Somehow three army officers were standing in front of Pat in his living room. Pat was frozen with a pair of pants in his hands. One of the officers was saying something Pat did not want to understand. Pat's arms were paralyzed. His lips miraculously formed words.

"I looked at them," he recalled, "and said, 'This has to be a

mistake. Casey has only been gone a couple weeks. This has got to be a mistake.'"[4]

Families know the drill when they see an army car outside their house. The army doesn't try to disguise its cars, but they are not all painted army green anymore. The license plates are government issue and offer a clue of official business. Parents sometimes run from the cars that pull into their driveways, hoping to escape the inevitability of death that has taken their child. Maybe if they don't hear the words, they won't be true. Their baby will come home and be okay and eat at the dinner table and laugh.

After she saw the army vehicle, Cindy pushed herself and made it inside. The three army officers still stood in her living room.[5] Her eyes went to her husband. Pat looked frozen. He had the pants in his hand but made no motions to put them down, fold them, or throw them. One of the officers repeated the message of Casey's death in Iraq.

Cindy collapsed. She wailed. The noises of mourning, fear, hate, and terror were so strange she didn't recognize they came from her soul.

"After what seemed like eternity, I finally began to wonder who or what was making those horrible screaming noises. Then I realized it was I. It couldn't have been Casey's father, because he was paralyzed in stunned silence holding the pair of pants he had been folding when the deliverers of death news arrived," Cindy later wrote.[6]

Her daughter, Carly, wrote a poem about Casey's death and Cindy's broken heart: "Have you ever heard the sound of a mother screaming for her son?" She says that it's comforting to hear others call Casey a hero, but accolades are lost amid the screams of her mother's heart. Screams that just won't stop

because the wound is too deep. It began in her womb and opened into her guts. Finally, it tore her heart.

Cindy walked through the motions of life, but she didn't feel alive.

"Then it was 10 days of agony before we buried him and then everyday is full of pain and emptiness," Cindy said.[7]

JAN WOKE up Monday morning and went back to the television in the front room. She flipped to CNN then to Fox News. Back and forth. She searched for something, anything, a sign that Justin was still alive. The news gave her nothing.

The hours between Rome, Georgia, and Iraq are hard to figure out when you're tired from war. Soldiers grab a phone when they can, and sometimes that can mean the middle of the night back home.

About midday on April 6, Jan's phone rang.

"Hi, Mom—I just wanted to let you know that I'm okay."

It was Justin. Jan could hear the exhaustion and fear coming through the lines that stretched thousands of miles. But her baby's voice was there. Live.

"Thank God," Jan said. "I've been watching the TV and seen all hell was breaking loose."

"I phoned you before, but they cut the lines 'cause of what happened."

"Why? What happened?"

"We lost some guys," Justin said. His soldier voice was starting to crack.

Justin broke. He wept as he told his mother about the guys who were pinned down inside Sadr City and how they called for reinforcements and the backups were too late. He tried to

help, and the terrorists shot at him. He was too late, and those filthy, faceless fiends killed his friends.

When a soldier dies, telephone communications back home are cut off. This gives the military time to notify families before the word spreads. The military is forced to race the split-second media who are on casualties like raptors. The army aims to notify the next of kin within four hours, but that doesn't always work out.

"Mom, I lost a good friend," he said. He tried to buck up. But the tears ran out of him.

"Remember the mechanic who worked on the Honda?"

He didn't tell her the soldier's name.

Jan knew it was Casey Sheehan.

2

JUSTIN'S DECISION

I asked my son not to go. I said, "You know it's wrong. You know you're going over there. You know your unit might have to kill innocent people. You know you might die."

—Cindy Sheehan[1]

Joe never once let it enter his mind that Justin wouldn't come home.

—Jan Johnson

R OME, GEORGIA, IS A cozy town in Floyd County where if the police nail you for speeding, your wife will likely know about it before you make it home. The Mayberry-like town is sixty-five miles northwest of Atlanta, in a valley hugged by the foothills of the Blue Ridge Mountains and the Appalachians.

Locals will tell you that God blessed Rome with the finest folks of the South—as well as the best fishing and hunting spots. The state fish is the largemouth bass, which tastes great when its battered up and fried. Three rivers cross Rome: the Coosa, Etowah, and Oostanaula. Cherokees called the area "the enchanted land" likely due to the fact that they didn't have to worry about food, thanks to the abundant wildlife.

Most folks who populate the small towns of Floyd County and a few of the larger ones like Rome (population thirty-six

thousand) can trace their family roots back for generations. You might call them homefolk because they don't move around a lot. They stick close to their families, because families hot-glue everyone together. Five mortuaries serve the folks in Rome, where burying the dead is a high honor.

If you aren't homegrown or have kin who drew you to Rome, you probably came for the beauty. The town is paradise for outdoorsmen and nature lovers. It touts the only "natural forest within a city limits in the United States," according to Romegeorgia.com.

God, family, and country are tattooed on the Romans' hearts and patriotism runs through their veins. A banner headline on the city Web site in July 2006 said, "Stand tall and proud, America. Some have short memories."

Romans don't forget any drops of blood spilled by their neighbors and family members in uniform. When a soldier dies, walls of homefolk, chests out, line the road to the cemetery during funeral processions. Newborn babies go to the parades of heroes so they can learn the right way to show love of country and its protectors. Kin and strangers alike bring out potato salads, pecan pie, peach cobbler, and fried green tomatoes for mourners at wakes. Folks usually encounter cousins and uncles who come to pay their respects.

The homegrown folks don't run away from Georgia's Confederate history. Nothing to be ashamed of here. Georgia joined the Confederacy on January 19, 1861. Looming in the face of nearby Stone Mountain are the figures of Confederate President Jefferson Davis and Gens. Robert E. Lee and Thomas J. "Stonewall" Jackson. Lee's beloved horse, Traveller, is also part of the world's largest sculpture. During the Civil War, Union Gen. William Tecumseh Sherman and his troops captured and

occupied Rome for six months. When they left, they burned much of the city to the ground, except for the hospitals. Rome rose again on the backs of its citizens who loved the valleys, hills, and all of the war dead in their cemeteries.

Georgia is a state of tough but polite people who can rustle up a mean streak if you challenge their independence. Up in the Rome cemetery, Civil War soldiers lie among the martyrs of other wars, and Confederate statues keep watch over the graves. Every war America has fought has included Rome residents in uniform. After September 11, 2001, men like the Johnson boys marched down to the local recruiting office and proudly scratched their names on the government forms to enlist.

Several hundred churches in Floyd County have taken out mortgages or launched fund-raising drives to build or maintain their gothic spiraled structures or the more modest endeavors that include four walls and a simple altar, decorated by pansies and tulips. After church on Sundays—or any time somebody's hankering for restaurant fixin's, Rome turns out to its favorite restaurants like Sonny's Real Pit Bar-B-Q or the best steak place in town, Country Gentlemen's, which serves a highly demanded blackened prime rib. And, of course, there are the ubiquitous Waffle Houses.

Rome beckoned Joe and Jan Johnson in 1986, when Jan's brother said, "Come here, you'll find work." Construction jobs were drying up for Joe in Houston, Texas, and he needed to feed his expanding family. So the Johnsons packed up and road-tripped their way to the little town of Kingston, just outside Rome. Too small, they decided quickly. Rome is where they wanted to put down their roots. Back in the 1980s Rome was still quiet and still—it was a good place to raise kids. Joe and Jan, both Southerners by birth, were glad to be home after

traveling the world during Joe's youthful stints in the army and navy.

JAN'S INSIDES convulsed. Her son's friends were dead, gunned down in Baghdad's largest slum. She ached for Casey's family and felt she was breathing borrowed air. Her consciousness wouldn't let go of how Justin sounded so tired on the phone.

"Mom, things aren't good. It's scary. You wouldn't believe this place. It's messing with our heads.

"Mom, you just never know. There are kids, ten- to twelve-year-olds and they got machine guns. You don't know: are they friendly or are they the enemy?"

Easter was five days away. Jan wasn't planning anything big at home because Joe and her children were out of town. Joe's brother decided to have an Easter egg hunt for the kids on Saturday. He lived in Armuchee, Georgia (the locals call it Arm-ur-chee), which is a fifteen-minute drive from Rome. Jan didn't feel much like dressing up and celebrating, though she figured she'd go to church with her friends. Everything was tinted with a dark veil of dread. It wasn't the jitters you would expect of a woman whose son is in a war zone and whose husband is waiting to go. That kind of fear rattles you out of the clear blue but allows you to go through the motions of life. This fear was different. It was manic, like a crazy woman on the street yelling about the end of the world.

What really spooked Jan was the last time she had seen her son.

Justin tried getting his things in order before he shipped out to Iraq. At Fort Hood, Texas, he packed stuff he didn't need and put it in storage. He took his truck and clothes to his par-

ents' home in Rome. His bedroom was in the back of his folks' double-wide. That was good by his mom, who didn't care for his shoddy housekeeping habits. She could just close the door and pretend the mess wasn't there.

Justin was biting at the bit to get to Iraq and fight. His unit, the First Battalion, Eighty-second Field Artillery Regiment, First Cavalry Division, was jerked around a few times. His unit of the First Team, as First Cavalry is known, was set to deploy, then plans changed for some bureaucratic reasons. It took a year before they received orders that would stick.

After Justin unloaded his clothes at home, Jan volunteered to drive him to the airport in Atlanta. The drive usually takes two hours—if you do the speed limit—so they would get plenty of time to talk or just ride together. Justin didn't like to talk much, but his mother could fill the airtime. While he was stationed at Fort Hood, Justin called home three or four times a day. He and his mom were close, so they really didn't have to say a thing to be comfortable together.

Justin was dog-tired. He stayed up most of the night with friends who sent him off with a party. Some old drinking buddies from high school showed up. He figured it was a good time to ask his girlfriend, Shannon, to marry him. They'd had some rough spots in their relationship and a breakup or two, but Justin loved his girl. He didn't have a ring for her, but he gave his word. When it came time for Justin to leave the party, Shannon begged him to stay. But he was tired and needed to get himself together. When he finally took off, he left Shannon on the couch, huddled in the fetal position.

Jan wasn't ready for Justin to go either.

They got into his 1995 black Honda Civic and headed toward Atlanta.

"I guess it was a good thing it was night, because I cried my eyes out," Jan said.

The dark couldn't hide her torment. Justin knew his mom was crying. He had some things to say that might hurt more, but Justin had to say them.

"Mom, if something happens to me, I want you to know I took care of you," he said, his own voice cracking. "I got insurance and stuff, and I want you to buy yourself a brand-new car. But don't get a convertible—Jordan doesn't need to be riding around in a convertible."

Jordan is Justin's firstborn niece, a rocket of a child with model-blonde hair and come-and-get-me eyes.

"Justin just thought there wasn't nothing better than her," Jan said.

If he had money to spend, he always thought of Jordan. When a new Polaroid-type camera came out, he spent the last of his money on film and snapped every picture of Jordan, who was two at the time. Justin and Joshua bought miniature army fatigues for her. Jordan and Justin posed for pictures in the uniforms, both of them smiling like it was V-E Day. An eight-by-ten of the portrait hangs in the Johnsons' front room.

Jan didn't want to talk. She might give herself away. Justin didn't need to hear her crying. She steadied her voice and promised she would not buy a convertible. The car would be safe for Jordan. She hated to talk like her boy wouldn't come home from the war. It felt wrong, like condemning him to death.

They sat silent for a while.

When they pulled into the airport, Justin told his mom to drop him off at the curb. No reason to park and go inside. He would leave soon. Jan didn't want to let him out. She wanted to pull him to her chest, hug him. But Justin was pumped, he was

so ready to pack a rifle into combat and fight next to his army buddies.

"I love you, Mom."

"I love you, Justin."

She let him go.

"I know it sounds weird, but I knew I'd never see him again," Jan said.

EVER SINCE Casey's death and Justin's phone call, Jan was out of sorts. She talked to her husband on the phone quite a bit and he tried to calm her. Nothing worked. How was she supposed to feel good? Her son was fighting terrorists who didn't mind blowing themselves up with bombs; her other son was preparing for deployment to Afghanistan; and her husband was recovering from an injury and hoped to go to Iraq. Thank God her daughter and grandkids were nearby.

Saturday rolled around and she was supposed to go to the Easter egg hunt and dinner. Maybe others could get her mind off the war, distract her from the habitual thoughts of Justin dodging bullets and roadside bombs. Things wouldn't be so bad if Justin were fighting a conventional enemy with uniforms. But the terrorists in Iraq hid bombs in garbage bags and dirt piles and animal carcasses so they could kill Americans as they traveled the roadways.

"They are spineless cowards. They don't fight like men— they don't look you in the eye," Jan said.

Jan rode with her daughter, Joleen, to Uncle Tim's five-acre place in Armuchee. Jordan couldn't wait to hunt the eggs and run around the yard on her toddler legs. About ten kids usually hunt, and the degree of difficulty increases with age. Uncle Tim

puts eggs in trees for the bigger boys, and there are plenty on the ground for the youngsters to gather. All in all, it takes about thirty minutes for the kids to pick the grounds of every colored-plastic egg. They work like locusts.

Just as Joleen pulled into the driveway at Tim's place, Jan was overwhelmed with nausea. Waves of poison seemed to rush through her insides, directed from some alien nerve center. "I just felt different. There was something wrong." She wanted to go home but wouldn't disappoint Jordan or the others. The weather was mild, in the seventies, and perfectly calm—great for egg hunting and gathering with the family.

Easter dinner with the Johnsons is always a good time. In the dictionary under "feast" you can find a description of the sit-down affair. Southerners don't cut corners on butter or cream or sugar. If you're hankering for some fried chicken, then get ready with the napkins. Easter dinner was extra special. Jan just didn't have the stomach for it.

Praying to God when you know your son is dead seems fruitless. God doesn't often raise people from their graves these days. There is nobody more alone in the world than a mother who knows the unbearable truth before anybody tells her. Maybe God gives her cloaked hints because she needs to start letting go before anybody else. It isn't easy to release a piece of your being, the flesh and blood your body gave to the world. Mary, the mother of Jesus, knew her son would die. She couldn't stop her soul from weeping.

Joleen took her mother home. She was worried about Jan, who was usually a good eater but only picked at her dinner that night. Nothing was going to work for Jan's stomach. Her body would repel anything. Jan didn't want to sleep in her bed. It wasn't right. Nothing was right. Jan wanted out of her skin,

which seemed too restricting. She sat in a recliner, waiting on something. Waiting. God, she didn't know what was happening. At least prisoners on death row know when they're going to die. Her insides burned with bile. Nothing worked. She couldn't even vomit. Her own body betrayed her.

God help me.

Jan sat up all night. Her only company was the twenty-four-hour news.

EASTER MORNING'S sun was trying to wake the state of Georgia. About 5:30 in the morning, Col. Yvette Kelley received a call from work. She had orders to notify a family that their son had been killed in Iraq. Yvette needed a chaplain to accompany her to Rome. Capt. Antonio Magwood would spend Easter with Yvette announcing the death of Floyd County's first soldier to fall in Iraq. Both dressed in their Class A's, the army dress uniform: green jacket, tie, slacks, and shined shoes. They drove northwest toward Rome, a town whose military roots reach beyond the Civil War when the Confederacy was favored. About thirty thousand people live in the city that oversees the historical Myrtle Hill Cemetery, the final resting place of First Lady Ellen Axson Wilson, wife of President Woodrow Wilson and 377 Civil War soldiers who died in battles around Rome.

Jan pulled herself out of the easy chair. Her body was still at war with her, but she knew she couldn't go much more if she didn't get something in her. She tried to eat a piece of dry toast, but the intensity of her sour insides festered. Jan always had a strong will, and she would need every ounce of that fortitude to make it to church. She went regularly, and it would be a sin to skip services on Resurrection Day.

Her friends Kricket and Chuck would pick her up in time for 9:00 a.m. Sunday school. Easter services at Rome Church of God began at 10:15. Jan struggled to get herself together. She didn't want anybody worrying about her. She didn't even know what to tell them when they asked what was wrong. Her buddies' black Pathfinder stopped at her trailer, and Jan climbed into the backseat. The sky was trying to turn blue for Easter, but it was drizzling in Atlanta.

The North Rome Church of God sits on Broad Street, a main artery for the town. The Pentecostal-charismatic congregation worships in an open sanctuary flooded in light green carpet with matching pews. Everything is easy on the eyes here at North Rome Church of God. The church has a Web site that explains its basic beliefs and its missions, which include evangelizing and building homes in third-world countries. Joe and Jan were missionaries for the church until Joe signed up for the army.

The Web site says this about the church's beliefs:

We believe that because of sin, a great chasm existed between God and humankind, so great that humankind could not make their way to God because of the great separation of sin. When Jesus the Christ, the Son of the Living God came, he provided for humankind a way back to God. He provided a bridge that crossed the great divide between God and humankind. He lived a sinless, perfect life and gave himself for a sacrifice for sin. He died for humankind and rose again on the third day so that we might have life with God the Father once again.[2]

Sunday services are broadcast on local radio station WRGA 1470.

Jan had no patience for Sunday school or church that day. Her toddler granddaughter would've lasted longer without wiggling and letting her thoughts drift to other dimensions. The sickness flooded Jan's brain and poisoned her nerves; she couldn't stop her body from acting out.

"I wanted to go home. I kept wishing this would be over," Jan said.

Jan prayed that the sermon would end.

"C'mon preacher man. Get it done. C'mon preacher," Jan said over and over in her head.

Everybody else followed the sermon with "amens" and "hallelujahs." Pretty pink hats and shiny shoes blended with the light green of the church. Jan wanted out. After services, she didn't want to hug people or smile and exalt in the Savior's resurrection. Chuck and Kricket wanted to go out for lunch, but Jan asked to go home.

When they pulled into the mobile-home park, Jan began to weep. She saw an army vehicle and two soldiers in their dress uniforms at her in-laws' place, which wasn't far from hers. Chuck stopped his Pathfinder, and Yvette asked him to pull around to Joe and Jan's mobile home. Yvette had memorized her speech, "The Secretary of the Army has asked me to express his deep regret . . ." Chuck stopped in front of Jan's home. Jan got out of the SUV and looked Yvette square in the eyes.

"Is Justin dead?" she asked.

Yvette's practiced speech failed her. She asked Jan to go inside, but Jan was having none of it. She had waited for this, the brutal truth. *Now tell me. Just tell me.*

"Is Justin dead?"

"Yes ma'am," Yvette replied.

Jan later found out the details of Justin's death. A roadside

bomb had ripped through his Humvee. He was on a mission in Sadr City, where Casey Sheehan had been killed six days earlier. A piece of shrapnel cut into Justin's side where the flack jacket didn't protect him. Justin was tall and thin, so the jacket was a little short when he bent over.

Justin bled to death at the very hour his mom fell ill.

The waiting was over. Jan had to act. She had to get to Joe. Yvette was trying to notify him, but she was getting nowhere. Joe was still in Fort Lewis, getting ready for assignment to Iraq, where he planned to join Justin and somehow watch his back. The way he saw it, you don't let your boy go to a war that you aren't willing to fight.

Jan called her husband on a cell phone. She tried to keep it together, but the tsunami of grief crushed her. The bile rushed out of her eyes and her mouth and her pores. Words got stuck in her throat. Her body was not fighting against her; it was trying to protect her from shock. Numbness had not set in yet.

"I had a hard time understanding her," Joe said.

Kricket took the phone and told him that Justin was dead—killed in Iraq. The information hit Joe like a torpedo.

"You have got to be kidding me," he said.

He was alone in his dorm, watching one of Justin's tapes, *Band of Brothers,* an HBO miniseries about paratroopers in World War II. He would never watch it again. Joe's roommate, a soldier from Kentucky, wasn't home. Anger immediately fired into him, roaring from his soul. It spewed from him in foul words, language that would make him ashamed if his head were straight. Jan wept uncontrollably. Her youngest child was dead, and she couldn't hold her husband.

"After I calmed down a bit, and he calmed down some, we then got back on the phone with one another and tried to make

some arrangements," Jan said. "He had to talk to his commanding officer and try to get things going on his end to have emergency leave and to get Red Cross or someone to fly him home. We sure didn't have any money since he had just left here a few days before that."

Joe and Jan made plans and said good-bye. Jan had to call her and Joe's families to tell them about Justin. Joe went straight to the small store on base and bought himself a six-pack of Budweiser and some Marlboro lights. He needed to numb his body and his mind. Alcohol was an old crutch. He spent eighteen years getting drunk early in his marriage, but he hadn't had a sip of booze for nine years. The phone call knocked him off the wagon. The beer kept Joe sufficiently buzzed to survive the shock of his child's death. *I wasn't there to protect him,* he kept repeating to himself. When the numbness gave way to the overwhelming darkness that made him cold and mad and scared, Joe thought about ending it all.

"I just wanted to crawl in a hole," he said. "To be honest, I think I would have taken a bottle of pain pills if I still had enough. The doctor gave me some pills for my knee. But there wasn't enough left to do it."

The buzz of the beer and nicotine didn't put Joe out of his misery or dull his nerves enough to forget his twins, Joshua and Joleen, or his grandchildren or Jan.

"He called home several times over the day, checking on me and the family," Jan said.

The Johnson family swarmed to Jan's side; the media weren't far behind. Justin was the first casualty for Floyd County, and the newspapers and television had to have the story. When an Atlanta reporter sat with Jan as she talked about Justin, Joe's brother came in and cussed President Bush.

Somebody was going to get the blame, and it might as well be Justin's commander-in-chief.

"He was ranting and raving," Jan said. "Then he saw that I wasn't blaming the president, and he figured, 'If she ain't blaming him, and she's the mom, then what am I doing?' He stopped."

Numbness finally settled Jan's body so she could survive. She hung in the classic first stages of grief. Anger had not welled in her. She understood the military; her husband had been a soldier when they were newlyweds. Still, nothing could steel her for this loss. Comfort caressed her, momentarily, when she thought of Justin's love and tenacity and energy when he left for war.

"I couldn't blame President Bush or anybody," Jan said. "This was Justin's decision."

AMERICAN SOLDIERS

I think he felt a sense of duty after what they did to us on September 11.

—*Joe Johnson on why his son joined the army*

The first chance he got, my brave, wonderful, faithful, sweet, gentle, and kind boy volunteered for a rescue mission as a combat life saver.

—*Cindy Sheehan on her son Casey*[1]

W HEN JUSTIN WAS A first-grader, his class had a career day where kids looked to their future. They got to dress up in nurse's outfits, cowboy hats—whatever they would wear in their chosen career. Justin wore his father's army camouflage.

"He put on Joe's shirt and hat," Jan said. "It looked like a tent."

Justin was like a lot of boys who think their dads are heroes. He was born in a navy hospital and grew up around men and women with a Southerner's love of country. An army uniform was a natural fit for the boy. Still, Jan figured his choice for career day wasn't so much prophetic as it was a badge of boyish dreams.

"I think he just liked the uniform," she said.

Justin didn't focus on the army as a career, mostly because

he was having too much fun running around Georgia, digging up Civil War artifacts in the red-clay dirt and wrestling with his dad. He wasn't afraid of much and challenged any and all authority. Justin was as quiet as the water moccasins that swam in the creeks of his youth. His thoughts were hard to figure out sometimes because his words were rare.

"Even when we were with all of our friends, he was the quietest person in the group," Justin's older brother, Joshua, said.

Joshua and his twin sister, Joleen, were born a couple years before Justin, which might account for some of Justin's tenacity and bullheadedness. Joshua was bigger and older and more experienced. All the way through first grade, Justin was the smallest in the class. He made up for it in speed and what you could call the roadrunner-coyote effect. Street smarts count for a lot when you have a big brother who really is big. Joshua was six feet two inches tall and weighed 240 pounds as a high-school senior. Full grown, Justin topped out at about six feet and 150 pounds or so—and that was after basic training where he put on 10 pounds. If two boys butting heads weren't enough, Joe tossed his hat into the ring for extra measure. He was smaller than Josh, so Joe would take his son down every once in a while just to maintain the rule of the roost.

"My boys had the testosterone thing going on," Jan said.

Competition ran like a wild boar in the Johnson home. Whether it was football or shooting a rifle, the Johnson boys measured themselves by how well they could whup each other. Justin had an eye for detecting things on the ground. Ever since he was a towheaded toddler with wild curls, he could find four-leaf clovers in any patch of green and always collected the most Indian arrowheads when he and his dad went hunting for them. Once while he was waiting for a school bus, he looked

down and found a steel ball used for ammunition in the Civil War.

"I told him he found stuff better than me because he was closer to the ground," Joe said. "Then he grew up taller than me, so I didn't have that excuse."

Justin's adventures started early and got bigger as he grew into his teenage years. He joined a club at Armuchee High School that specialized in thrill-seeking. It was a science club that took the teens to unusual spots for study, such as caves. Justin started spelunking when he was about ten years old. When the Armuchee science club went caving, Justin helped his teacher guide the other students. He was built like his father: lean, scrappy, and strong as an ox on steroids. Justin had about as much fear as a bull in a field of hornless cows.

Caving isn't for sissies or anybody with even a hint of claustrophobia. Justin enjoyed the challenge of tight spaces and darkness. He and Joe spent hours exploring the caves and negotiating the water that ran through them like cut veins. Their favorite spot was Pettyjohn Cave in Lafayette, Georgia, a geological wonderland on the east side of Pigeon Mountain that is made mostly of limestone, sandstone, and shale. Water flows through the cave from streams and rain sources that can make it a muddy, dangerous place. Mysteries of the cave draw adrenaline junkies to the not-so-benign Pettyjohn. The danger is so real that teams from the Georgia Department of Natural Resources have trained specifically to rescue folks from the cave, such as a twenty-year-old man who damaged his spine while spelunking at Pettyjohn.[2] Folks have died in the cave's dark arms and creeping arteries. Injuries and the threat of death did not deter Justin—they were more likely to lure him.

"He was our daredevil," Jan said.

Justin took his lead from his dad and uncles, who revved their fight-or-flight adrenaline by jumping out of perfectly good airplanes.

"Joe and his brothers were the first to do the skydiving—Justin just watched for several months till he was old enough, then made his first jump on his sixteenth birthday," Jan said. "Josh has the video of it at his house."

As soon as he could walk, Justin ran. When he could swim, he dove. Justin devoured the earth, the sky, and the blue and muddy water. Life would not get away from him. He mimicked his dad, learning to aptly swing a journeyman's hammer when he was only three. Justin climbed on roofs with no fear of falling and dived deep into the ocean with no fear of losing air.

Scuba diving was a family thing. Joe, Jan, and Justin learned the tricks of breathing from a tank while underwater at the YMCA. Their foreign exchange student, Chris, also took the classes and earned certification for open-water divers. The family went to the Florida Keys twice to explore the underwater world. Justin was sixteen.

"He did live a full life. He did things eighty-year-old guys have never done," Jan said. "As far as adventure, there wasn't much he wanted to do that he didn't do."

Justin faced murky caves with no sun, the wind with no wings, and the ocean with only canned air. Yet he never spoke of great fear—until he went to Iraq.

☆ ☆

SEPTEMBER 11, 2001. Radical Muslims hijacked planes and used them as weapons of mass destruction, flying the fuel- and passenger-loaded airbuses into the twin towers of the World Trade Center in New York City and the Pentagon in Washington,

D.C., and crashing one in a Pennsylvania field. Justin was working at the family business. His sister, Joleen, heard about the attacks on the radio while she was driving to Joe and Jan's place.

"I was on the way over to their house to give help, say bye and everything, because they were going to Ecuador for three months on a mission trip," Joleen said. "And I was drivin' down the road and all of a sudden it said that a plane had hit one of the Twin Towers. 'What?!' I said, 'It's gotta be a radio hoax.' Because they do them all the time here, stuff like that. And then a few minutes later, it said the other one had been hit. And I was like, 'This can't be!'"

Joleen got to her mom's and told Jan about the planes. Jan didn't have cable yet, so they called Grandma, and she checked it out. "Yeah, I'm seein' it right here on TV!"

"And Dad was saying, 'You know, if they can do that, they can put a plane in the Pentagon.'" Joleen recalled. "And a few minutes later, the Pentagon had been hit."

Justin came home later "and that's when he thought he was goin' in the army," Joleen said. "He said something about how we needed to fight back."

Two weeks later, Justin took another step toward his goal to fight as a soldier.

"I went to the recruiter yesterday," he told Joleen.

"You're jokin'."

"No, I went and talked to the recruiter yesterday. I'm thinkin' about joinin' the army. I want Dad to hurry up and come home."

Jan and Joe were in Ecuador working at an orphanage as part of a mission for the Church of God. Justin hounded his sister and parents to help him sign up for the army. Joe had already served, so he knew how to deal with military contracts

and recruiters. Justin was enraged that radical killers had attacked America. He wanted to defend the United States against her enemies.

"He wanted to go because it was going to be an adventure," Joe said. "And he was so excited about getting a combat patch, you know. I think it was a sense of duty."

Joe was torn about his son's joining the army. He knew combat was in the cards because the war on terror could be endless. But never—never—did he think Justin would die in the war. The Johnsons and the Bunces (Jan's family) have fought in wars since America's first days. They took up both sides of the Civil War. Not one fell in combat.

"You know, sometimes I ask myself, did I try hard enough to keep him out of the military? Because I tried to talk him out of the job that he wanted, which is forward observer, and we argued several times over it, and he was adamant about wanting to do that," Joe said. "And I told him, 'Justin, that's a very dangerous job. A forward observer is just one step above being in the infantry. And sometimes it's worse than that, because you're out in front of the infantry.' But that's what he wanted to do, which, I don't think I'd ever talked him out of it, you know, for the dangerous aspect of it, because that's what he wanted. He liked doing things that were dangerous, like scuba diving, skydiving, going in caves."

It was also the job that Joe took when he was in the army years before.

Justin had other reasons besides the September 11 attack to sign with the army. He never planned to be a lifer, but the armed forces seemed like a good fit for a wild man whose guns might as well have been attached to his body at birth, like arms or legs.

Justin had a job with his father and mother's home-building company, Johnson Construction. Sometimes working with family gets messy with emotions and high expectations. The boss is your dad, and your boss doesn't buy your hogwash.

"We'd get in fights, and Justin would leave or I'd fire him," Joe said. "I must've fired him a couple times."

A man and his son have a lot to fight about. Partying all night then showing up late isn't a good way to start a day—even if your dad used to do the same thing when he was your age. Stumbling into work with booze on your breath will not earn brownie points with the old man. Justin pushed the envelope—and his father's nerves—in work as much as in play. Defending the country seemed like a good idea. Besides, packing a .50-caliber gun for the army geared Justin's adrenaline more than swinging a hammer for his Dad.

"I really don't know the reasons he joined the army, but I'm guessing a new career was a big part of it," his brother said. "He did not enjoy working construction with our family. I think he was just looking for a change."

Once Justin got his contract with the army signed, he went to Fort Sill in Oklahoma for basic training and advanced individual training. This is where the army takes conceited, over-confident smart alecks who think they can conquer the world with their own wit and turns them into conceited, overconfident smart alecks who can conquer the world with the might of the U.S. Army behind them. The Web site for Fort Sill warns: "Basic Combat Training is extremely rigorous. The Drill Sergeants take every available opportunity to teach and mentor the young soldiers they have been charged with." In other words, you are so screwed, maggot.

Soldiers go through three phases of training at Fort Sill. First

is the Red-Patriot Phase that includes initial values training, physical training, inspections, drill and ceremonies, general subjects (map reading, communications, first aid, and other mandatory classes), and bayonet training (assault course/pugil training/bouts).

Next up is the White-Gunfighter Phase where you learn to love your weapons more than your momma. Here you get basic rifle marksmanship, more on values and first aid, and a good test of physical fitness and hand-to-hand combat. If you survive that, the soldier-in-training moves on to the Blue-Warrior Phase where the army gives you some confidence training and live-fire practice, among other handy warrior training. Soldiers come out of the training and move on to more specialized stuff for their military occupational specialty (MOS), which is your job.

Joining the army isn't like the good old days when enlistment was viewed as an option for teenagers facing punishment for various misdemeanor and misdeeds. Today's army doesn't want anybody who's fat, tattooed with gang graffiti or anything else that offends, or has been on medications such as Ritalin, which is used to treat attention deficit disorder and other disabilities.[3]

Justin faced a female drill sergeant who was lucky if she was tall enough to stare at his chest, but she was meaner than a hungry bear just out of hibernation. She cussed him and challenged his manliness. It was almost like getting his butt kicked inside out every day. As her spittle shot from her foul mouth, it couldn't connect any higher than Justin's neck—if she were stretching it. There were no eye-to-eye stare downs like you see in the movies when the drill sergeant lays into a skin-headed soldier.

"She was a real witch," Justin told his mom.

The drills worked. Justin came out of basic with stubble on his head and the army in his heart.

During advanced individual training (AIT), Justin blew the competition back on the rifle range. His days spent hunting alongside his Dad and uncles in Georgia served him well. In one session, every shot hit the bull's-eye.

"You ever seen anything like that before?" one drill sergeant asked another.

"Yep. I did it myself," the other answered.

Justin later told his mom about how the shooting thrilled his drill sergeant. The army considered sending him to sniper school, but during another test, he messed up on the range on a windy day. Still, those sergeants couldn't get enough of the boy from Georgia.

"They were all the time kidding Justin and the other boys from the South that they could always depend on them to do good at the ranges because they knew they grew up with a deer rifle in their hands," Jan said.

Gun handling comes in handy when you're in a war zone.

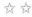

CASEY SHEEHAN was born in Southern California on Memorial Day, May 29, 1979. His mother had a difficult labor that lasted long enough to flatten Casey's head as he moved through her birth canal. Casey's parents called him Edward G.,[4] which was short for Edward G. Robinson, the Hollywood actor known for his depiction of gangster boss Rico Bandello in *Little Caesar* (1930). Casey's parents took him to church and had him baptized a Catholic. The religion would become part of Casey's being.

"Everyone assumed Casey was going to be a priest, because

he was so faithful to his God and to his church," his mother wrote.[5] "He never missed Mass, even when he went into the army."

Pat and Cindy loved listening to their baby boy coo and play in his crib. For the first few months of his life, Casey slept in his parents' bedroom.

"Casey was a very good baby. From the time he was about seven months old and had gone into his own room, he would wake up in the morning and talk to himself and play with his crib gym. His dad and I would lie in our room and listen to him play," Cindy wrote.[6]

When Casey was old enough for school, Pat and Cindy enrolled him at a Catholic school. He made an impression on the other students who, years later, remembered the religious little boy who grew up to be one of the most famous soldiers from the Iraq War.

"Casey, I remember you from back in the day at St. John of God School. We were in the basketball team together, and I remember you making it to a free-throw contest. It surprised me that you made it, but I was proud of you. I'm proud of you now of what sacrifice you have done, not for yourself, but for others. My prayers are always with you and your family," classmate Mark Poblete wrote.[7]

When he was old enough to hold a wrench, Casey and his father worked on old cars together. Whether out of necessity or just out of a love of automobiles, the two became master mechanics and body specialists. The skills helped Casey when he joined the service, though his first choice was not working on cars for the army. In fact, his mom was surprised when he signed up to wrench on Humvees because she said that he didn't even want to work on his own jalopy.

Casey wanted to be a chaplain's assistant—not a stretch of the imagination for a young boy who used to fashion towels into priest vestments and play church Mass with his siblings. He, of course, was the priest. Despite the benign nature of spreading the word of the Lord and counseling distressed soldiers, a chaplain's assistant can be a lethal job; the army classifies it as a combat position. Chaplains don't carry sidearms or any weapons to protect themselves. That's the job of the chaplain's assistant, who is bodyguard, buddy, and replacement for a chaplain if he goes down in combat. Army mechanics usually don't engage the enemy, because they are supposed to keep the war machines running. But every soldier knows he may face enemy fire.

Religious leaders have comforted warriors since the first war. The Bible describes priests going into battle alongside the troops: "And it shall be, when ye are come nigh unto the battle, that the priest shall approach and speak unto the people" (Deuteronomy 20:2).

Chaplains have saved soldiers' souls on and off every battlefield stained with American blood:

From 1775 to 1783 the chaplains' story parallels that of the Revolutionary Army. Between 222 and 238 served in the American cause. Chaplains were to be found in every campaign and on every battlefield in the long conflict: Bunker Hill, Quebec, White Plains, Trenton, Princeton, Brandywine, Saratoga, Monmouth, King's Mountain, Camden, Yorktown. Their duties were wide ranging, for besides accompanying the soldiers into battle and on the march, the trials of war found them preaching in camp, visiting and caring for the sick and wounded, and ministering to the dying. On 2 January 1777, John Rosbrugh was

killed in the second battle of Trenton, the first American chaplain killed during the Revolution.[8]

But Casey was not a chaplain or chaplain's assistant; he was a minister of the Catholic Church who could give Communion to soldiers in the field. This communing with God would be especially important to a dying Catholic soldier.

The Sheehans eventually moved to Vacaville in Solano County. The county has a long agricultural and military history. It proudly supported Mare Island Naval Base, one of the oldest naval bases in the country's history and the first on the West Coast. Workers at Mare Island launched its first ship, USS *Saginaw,* on March 3, 1859. The *Saginaw* was a wooden-hulled steamer with a side paddlewheel and four guns. Mare Island shipbuilders produced more than 500 ships in its 142-year history, including the first nuclear submarine out of the West Coast.

Shipbuilders from Vallejo were most proud of USS *Ward,* which they built in seventeen and a half days during World War I. The *Ward* fired the first U.S. shots of World War II, sinking a Japanese midget submarine just outside of Pearl Harbor. President Franklin Roosevelt visited Mare Island, cruising around the base in a convertible car to boost the morale of the hardworking shipbuilding crews, which included Rosie-the-Riveter types.

World War II also bolstered a second military base in Solano County, the Fairfield-Suisun Army Air Base. The name was later changed to Travis Air Force Base, which, in military terms, is now the "Gateway to the Pacific. " Travis—which is inside the city limits of Fairfield—handles more cargo and passengers than any other military air terminal in the United States.

During President Bill Clinton's adminstration, Mare Island

was closed, and the economy in southern Solano County hemorrhaged for years. Yet Mare Island has forever left a military flavor to Solano County, as has the now-extinct Benicia arsenal and the thriving Travis Air Base. Everybody in Solano County is either from a military family or knows one. Reagan Democrats live in Solano, though an influx of more liberal folks lately has changed area politics.

The Sheehans were not a military family, but flags flew on the homes surrounding them and patriotism ran through Casey. Casey's siblings attended Holy Spirit School in Fairfield while Casey went to Vacaville High School, where teachers and old classmates remember him as smart and quiet.

Casey joined the Cub Scouts when he was six years old and still living in Southern California. He stayed with the Boy Scouts once his family moved to Vacaville and aimed for the highest Boy Scout honor: Eagle Scout. By 1996—a year before graduating high school—Casey reached his goal by planting trees in the Table Mountains in the Angeles Forest. He was only the second scout in his troop to attain the rank.

Casey was eight when he began helping priests at Mass as an altar server. This is no easy task. Roman Catholics follow rituals that date back to the earliest days of the Christian church. Altar servers must know every nuance, every move, every prayer and special ceremony for Holy Days. Priests differ on how they want a book or challis held or where they want the altar servers to stand. Casey was always reverent and knew his religion as if it were passed to him through his Irish Catholic blood.

"Casey was righteous," said Liz Kroman, Cindy Sheehan's best friend and an art instructor at Holy Spirit School where Casey's siblings went to school. "He always felt the Holy Spirit within him."

When Father Benedict DeLeon was pastor of St. Mary's, he met Casey. Father Benedict considered Casey a close friend and a model Christian. Parishioners recognized Casey because he served at Mass, helped the youth group his mother operated, and became a Eucharistic minister, which means he could offer Communion to people inside the church or even at home if they were ill. St. Mary's hoped to operate an outdoor meeting place for youth on land that was donated to the church in Vacaville. Casey pitched in to transform the raw, wild land into a more hospitable spot.

"Casey did a lot of work," said Mary Ferrari, a close Sheehan friend.[9] "He was a very devout boy."

Casey was a loyal parishioner and worked as an altar server throughout his years in high school. After graduating, he finally asked his mother if it would be okay to become a lay minister instead of continuing as altar server. She said yes.

School kept Casey busy during his high-school years when he was determined to keep himself on the honor rolls. The school, whose mascot is the bulldog, offered distractions. Before the town had another high school, everybody was loyal to Vaca High. Businesses kept stickers on the doors saying "Push for the Bulldogs." Some still have the orange-and-black decals. For years Bulldog sports ranked right after God, country, and family as priorities with Vaca High students and alumni. Casey played ball when he was younger but preferred academics and theater in high school, appearing in the play *Good Morning Miss Dove,* a story about a New England schoolteacher who is confined to bed with illness and spends her days thinking about the students she taught over the years.

Casey's home was always full of young people from school or church. From the time he was born until he died, Casey was

close to his family. They did everything together, including bowling, going for yogurt, or watching movies at home. Casey graduated from high school with honors in 1997.

He moved on to college at Solano Community College, a two-year institution where he continued his studies in theater. He also wrote for the school's newspaper, doing reviews on theater. Mary Mazzocco was an adviser for the college newspaper.

"Casey was on the staff of the *Tempest* in spring 2000, the first semester we had the paper up and running again after a hiatus of about a year and a half," Mazzocco said. "He covered arts and entertainment, primarily, although he also was a huge fan of WWF and wrote a very favorable review of the Rock's autobiography for the paper."

Like his mother, Casey laughed with energy and lightness and booming sound. His smile widened and joy poured from him. Like his father, Casey was quiet most of the time—unless he had something important to share. Like both of his parents, Casey carried his love of God close to his soul.

"Anybody who knew Casey knew he was serious about his religion. But he wasn't an evangelist about it, and it wasn't the first thing you learned about him," Mazzocco added.

Politics was not a big distraction for Casey—even after he was old enough to join the army and vote. A registered Democrat like his mom, Casey had only voted once before he died.[10]

His college adviser saw Casey as a young man still searching for his fit in life, as are the majority of students at a community college. Neither she nor Casey's parents had a clue that he had considered enlisting in the army.

"Casey joined the army in May of 2000," Cindy said.[11] "I was devastated. He was 21, he didn't discuss it with us."

The family ached that Casey would move out of the home and perhaps face war. When he signed up, the World Trade Center still stood in New York. Americans did not know—or just didn't recognize—the evil that would change the country forever some sixteen months after Casey joined the army.

Four years after he signed his first contract with the U.S. Army, Casey decided to continue his stint and reenlisted. His mother was again shocked.

While the family had no signs of Casey's aspirations, he did speak to at least one person about his ideas. Back when he was in high school and thinking about his future, Casey had a chance meeting with an air force veteran at his home. It turned out to be a counseling session on the military.

Bob Freethy and Larry Niemotka went to the Sheehan home to check on its condition. The Sheehans were renting a house on Sunridge Street at the time, and the home's owner lived out of town. The owner asked Bob to stop by, and he invited Larry along. The Freethy family had met the Sheehans through Boy Scouts and knew them to be involved in their children's activities. Bob was shocked at what he saw.

Casey answered the door and didn't want to let the two men inside, but eventually he stepped aside. As they crossed the threshold, the stench of ammonia and burning candles almost knocked them over.

"It was like going into the SPCA," Bob said. "There wasn't one square-foot of the carpet that wasn't peed on."

Bob surveyed the house so he could report to the owner. The microwave was thick with filth, and the oven door was torn from its hinges. Blades from the overhead fan were missing and Casey said the kids had used them for a school project. The backyard was overgrown, the once-clean redwood deck was

now painted blue, and the pool was destroyed. "It looked like somebody had skateboarded in it," Bob said.

Some bedrooms upstairs had bare mattresses lying on the floor, Bob said. "They were the kids' rooms."

Larry went to the upper floor on the tri-level home. He poked his head into a bedroom and saw Casey.

"I noticed a guitar in the corner and I play the guitar, so we talked about that some," Larry said. (Casey's sister Janey plays the guitar).

Casey told him that he wanted to join the military when he graduated from high school. Larry served in the air force and told Casey to choose carefully which service to join.

"You are less likely to face combat if you join the navy than if you go to the army," Larry said. "He was serious about it, so I pointed that out to him. As far as I could determine, he looked at the military as a way to escape [the mess at home]."

Casey was feeling his way into his future. His college newspaper adviser saw a lot of that in healthy young adults who go through her classes.

"He was one of those students I would describe as searching for a good fit. It's pretty typical for his age to be trying out different things to see what works; the paper was something he was trying out. That was the one thing that made sense to me about his enlisting [in the army]; I thought it was part of his process of finding himself," Mary Mazzocco said.

Casey was gentle but strong. He stuck to his beliefs and was steadfast in his convictions, whether they dealt with the Catholic Church, the love of his family and country, or helping others who were in need or in trouble. His sister Carly is proud of her brother and understood how Casey could join the military.

"That's all he wanted to do was serve God and his country his whole life," she said. "He was a Boy Scout from age six or seven and an Eagle Scout. It was kind of a natural progression to go into the military from that. He said he was enjoying the military because it was just like the Boy Scouts but they got guns."[12]

BOYS AT
FORT HOOD

Justin used to talk to me about Casey and how he fixed the
car. They were buddies.

—*Jan Johnson*

I know one thing from the bottom of my heart. My son
Casey, who was an Eagle Scout and a true American patriot,
was not served well by his idea of patriotism.

—*Cindy Sheehan*

CASEY AND JUSTIN MET at Fort Hood, the mother of all army
bases near the booming town of Killeen, Texas. The 340-
square-mile complex has a southern personality that laughs in
the face of the wilting sun and quickly offers you a cold glass of
sweet tea. Men call Hood "the Great Place" because nothing
compares for a red-blooded soldier. A momma's boy could get a
real butt kicking here.

The base received its name from the colorful, nail-spitting
Confederate Gen. John Bell Hood, who was a Union officer in the
1850s but resigned his commission and joined the Confederate
army after the war-fueling attack on Fort Sumter. He commanded
the Texas Brigade during the Civil War and was so loyal to his
troops that, even after he lost his right leg, he strapped himself
into his saddle and continued leading his soldiers into battle.

Fort Hood is the only post in the United States that can support two armored divisions. Casey and Justin were part of the First Cavalry Division, the Texas fighting machine that has roots stretching back to America's first days. Some seventeen thousand soldiers now belong to the First Cav, whose alumni are proud of its heritage and brotherhood that includes American icon Elvis Presley.

When Casey shipped in to Fort Hood, he was already in pretty good shape. The quiet young man who had studied acting in college was transformed into a soldier at Fort Jackson, South Carolina, a vast, sandy spot with temperatures that are friendly to soldiers-in-training all year long. Fort Jackson was made for fine-tuning bodies and minds that protect the United States. Its own beginning traces back to when Maj. Douglas MacArthur told the country on May 19, 1917, that one of sixteen new cantonments would be built near Columbia, South Carolina. The country faced a conflict with the Central Powers in Europe and needed large training camps to get ready to defend herself.

Basic training was tough on Casey. He suffered stress fractures in his ankles. The army advised him to leave the service, but he wouldn't give up. He wanted to be a soldier.

Casey was more than six feet tall and wore lean muscle when he arrived at Fort Hood. A long line of Irishmen with fair skin and lots of backbone paved the way for Casey's life—so neither the heat of Texas nor the stringency of the army tired him much. He never shied away from a job that required pain and sweat, but he preferred acting and the quiet of a Catholic church.

When he signed his army contract and enlisted in May 2000, Casey took the job of a light-wheel mechanic. He also took a class on inserting IVs and treating trauma victims. One more step beyond the combat lifesaver training, and he could

have been a medic. He wanted to help his brothers and sisters if they fell in battle. Casey was always the first to help.

Casey and Justin hung out at Fort Hood's motor pool, the spot where the guys could talk and work on trucks. It was kind of like home. Justin had a 1995 Honda that liked breaking down. Casey worked the bugs out and saved Justin money he didn't have to spend.

The only time Justin didn't go to Casey for help on the Honda was when a topless dancer in Texas repeatedly kicked his car with her high heels to the tune of eight-hundred-dollars worth of dents. She was miffed because Justin had just beaten her boyfriend. Justin hadn't picked the fight, but he finished it. The boyfriend had just beat up Justin's buddy. Justin was nothing if he wasn't loyal, so he went after the guy. When he finished the fight and left the guy on the ground, the girl went wild. The exotic dancer got to kicking the car until it looked like a truck had broadsided it. Justin didn't ask Casey to fix the damage. As far as Justin's mom knows, the car still bears the scars of the dancer's fury.

Casey was older than Justin by a couple years. Both were tall, but Casey had more meat on his bones. Justin was a hair shorter than Casey, coming in at just below six feet. Quiet settled in them, but in different ways.

"I never saw Casey or Justin angry," said Levi Lohnes, an army buddy who knew both men at Fort Hood and in Iraq.

They were happy guys who loved a good joke, their family and friends. The two settled into their life at Fort Hood as well as any young men could. Buddies kept them busy, but the civilian life at home with families didn't seem so far away.

Justin called his mother back in Georgia sometimes four times a day. Casey tried to call his mother every day.

"When I first met Casey, the first thing he did was take me to some pictures he had there," Levi said.

"This is my family," Casey said.

"I never saw a guy do that before—first thing like that," Levi said.

Casey and Levi liked to walk around the Killeen Mall, which wasn't far from base. They would mostly window-shop, but Casey liked to buy comic books. Casey didn't like to party much. His buddies would catch him Sunday mornings when they were coming in from a night of drinking and Casey was on his way to Mass, his Bible in hand.

Justin also spent time with God, reading the Bible and going to services that weren't as structured as the North Rome Church of God back home. The music at the army services kept him coming back for more.

"We talked about our beliefs a lot. The first time that we ever did was when we had to go up to Fort Knox to train cadets from West Point," Justin's roommate Luke Herbst said. "He told me about how his parents were missionaries, and my sister at the time was one, so we connected on that level. We also knew once we got to Iraq there was a good chance that someone, maybe one of us, were not going to be coming back. So we both knew that we had to be right with the Lord when we got over there. When Justin and I were sharing that room in Iraq and we had downtime, he would be writing letters and reading his Bible. I think that that's just something that we both did every time that we had downtime."

Casey and Levi were neighbors in the barracks. Levi said,

Casey moved next door to me in the barracks in . . . 2001? . . . 2002? I think. It's all a blur now. I did the neighborly thing and

introduced myself, asking the usual questions. Where did you go to basic? AIT [advanced individual training]? Where are you from? Why the army? That kind of stuff.

I remember him saying he was from California and how he thought the army was a good way to help out with school. I agreed. We talked about what we wanted to do with our lives after we got out, and he surprised me by saying that his goal was to become an actor. It's not every day you meet a Joe with ambitions like that.

He showed me his room and the one thing I remember about it was the family picture he had on display. Most guys weren't close enough to their families or didn't bother with ornamental trinkets like that. His family even came out to see him when we were training up for Iraq in the Mojave Desert in 2003. We were impressed by this kind of affection because a lot of guys were from Cali[fornia], and Casey's was the only family to make the trip out there and see him.

We'd hang out and watch movies with a mutual friend after work some days, go get something to eat and hit a game store in the mall, or browse in this huge bookstore in the adjacent town of Killeen. Him and our friend Zeke were addicted to comic books.

He wasn't much into partying, so the only time I saw him on the weekends was when I'd trek down to the soda machine in a futile effort to cure a hangover on Sunday mornings. There were a number of times I'd pass him in the hall and say hi. I'd be walking like a zombie in my pajamas and he'd be on his way back from the post chapel in his Sunday clothes with Bible in hand. So it only made sense when I read that he was an honor student and an Eagle Scout in one of the stories that came out about him and Cindy.

He was the quiet type who was never one to make a scene. If I had to describe him professionally, I'd say Casey was a hard working, sharp, and dedicated soldier, too. Mechanics have it the worst as far as the hours they put into working on our vehicles (when we're in garrison), and I don't remember him ever losing his temper at work or in the barracks like most guys did if they had a bad day. He took everything in stride. He was also the kind of guy that would bend over backwards for you. I know he helped quite a few guys out if they ever had a problem with their cars. Casey was the one mechanic I could depend on back when we were privates and I was a Humvee driver. Most guys would be bogged down with other stuff and say they'd be there to help you out with your vehicle just to get you off their back (which is understandable). Not Casey. I usually only had to ask him once and he'd be there minutes later, ready to help me install a part or sign off on an inspection.

THEN CAME deployment to Iraq, referred to as "the sandbox" by the troops. When the devil lit up the dirt in Iraq, Casey put fear behind him and stepped up to a job he didn't have to take. Combat is not the number-one priority for mechanics, but saving another soldier was Casey's goal, one that sent him to Sadr City. And Justin followed.

5

SIX DAYS IN SADR

It made me do a lot of thinking. . . . It was hard knowing this
was where he died.

—*Joe Johnson on seeing Sadr City*

My firstborn was murdered. Am I angry? Yes, he was killed
for lies and for a PNAC Neo-Con agenda to benefit Israel.
My son joined the army to protect America, not Israel.

—*Cindy Sheehan*[1]

ON APRIL 4, 2004, a terrorist killed Casey Sheehan, forever
silencing the American soldier who sparked a mother's
march against the Iraq War. Cindy says she knows what Casey
would think of all of this: the war, her protests, even her hate of
his commander-in-chief. She believes that he would want the
United States to retreat.

Jan had no hate. How could she hate the war or President
Bush? If she did, then she faced the cruelty that her son had died
for nothing. But the crushing blows to her heart wouldn't stop.

A mother is haunted by her son's last breath. Anger jabs at
her heart and screams, "Why didn't you protect me?" The
mother's body answers in moans and screaming and, God will-
ing, finally numbness, so she can breathe. It is not natural for a
mother to bury her child.

God should have taken me instead.

The silent film rolls with imagined snapshots of her child's last minutes.

The last scent, sweet or decayed.

The last sight, light or hell.

Then the shot. The explosion.

SADR CITY is a steaming slum of humanity and its waste. Gutters run with human waste, urine, blood, and vomit. Trash grows in piles that stand as monuments of the poor who live in the sprawling Shi'ite slum. Carcasses of animals rot alongside roads and markets where Iraqis shop for fresh food. The smells attest to the city's history of hate and disregard for life. North of Baghdad, Sadr City's population includes descendants of Iraqi martyrs and veterans of the Iran-Iraq War that roared for eight years. The despair that breathes here flourished during Saddam Hussein's tyrannical reign when the city was called Saddam City. Families remember riots against Saddam that ended in lynchings and torture by the madman's henchmen.

After coalition forces took Baghdad in April 2003, Saddam City became Sadr City, named after Muhammad Sadiq al-Sadr, the ayatollah whose face appears in portraits around the city. His long face covered with a mask of snowy beard watches over the city in the same way that images of Jesus are sentinels for Christian homes. One year later, Justin and Casey saw nothing but fires brewing from hell. Sadr City's history—and its residents' loyalty to al-Sadr and his round-faced son Muqtada al-Sadr—are important to understanding why and how Casey died on Black Sunday and Justin fell six days later.

Sadr City is the ugly, bloody, starving stepchild of Baghdad.

It is a slum that rose from the desperation of destitute Shi'ite farmers who once lived in the countryside. It was originally created as a refuge and home for thousands of poor Iraqis with no ties to the country's power center. The Shi'ites turned to Communism, believing it would help them from their poverty, but it failed. Then came Ayatollah Muhammad Sadiq al-Sadr, who had studied under Ayatollah Ruhollah Khomeini, the force behind the Iranian Revolution. He had the gall to stand up to Saddam Hussein, and this gained him prestige and power among the poor masses.

The assassination of Ayatollah Muhammad Sadiq al-Sadr in 1999 sparked a massive mourning among the Shi'ites who showed up by thousands to pay respect and to violently protest the political killing. Saddam's government cracked down, with Baath officials and others firing into crowds of civilians. Victims lay around the city like ticker tape after a New York celebration.

The Baath Party for days continued its terrorism of the poor, arresting and executing innocents at will. Outrage and the quest to survive changed forever the hearts of the people living in the slums. Their loyalty to the al-Sadr family was seared into them like a brand. Who else would protect them from Saddam Hussein?

U.S. forces started out on the good side of Sadr City residents after the fall of Baghdad. The poor looked at the coalition troops as liberators and even heroes. After all, the Americans had come to depose Saddam. Things changed a year after the Americans appeared. The slum's people tired of the sight of armed soldiers in their neighborhoods—it felt like the old days of the Baath Party to some, even if there were no torture or threats. Old wounds festered, and Muqtada al-Sadr was smart

enough to exploit the fear. He would become their leader and enflame their darkest nightmares of invaders. The people of Sadr City wanted freedom and self-rule. Never would they make the mistake of laying down their swords against oppressors like Saddam.

Sadr's organization spurred the people to rabid protest, and the Coalition government, led by the Americans, shut down the group's newspaper, *al Howza,* for inciting violence. On April 3, 2004, an estimated ten thousand Sadr loyalists took to the streets in protest, some carrying automatic weapons and traditional war sickles. Snipers crawled the surrounding roofs.[2]

ON APRIL 4, 2004, replacement units were moving in to take over for the First Armored Division (1AD). The switch was not complete, though battalion commanders and officers had been in Iraq for about a month for training. Casey and Justin were among the thousands of soldiers to hit the war zone as replacements.

Black Sunday began with soldiers escorting crews dispatched to remove the raw sewage from Sadr City, hauling it away in what the soldiers call "honey wagons." Four Humvees pulled three honey wagons. The natives didn't seem to care that the soldiers were there to help them with the sewage problem, which overpowered the slum with its stench and maggots. Iraqis threw rocks at the soldiers working in the streets and began threatening the Americans with death. The patrol next ran into problems when armed men took cover in a mosque and refused to give up their weapons. A gunshot pierced the thick air—the first to discharge in what would become the most brutal battle in Iraq since the first days of the war—and the last day of Casey's life.

As the soldiers moved through the town, the air blackened with the toxic smoke of burning tires. Sadr's followers used the garbage that defined their town as roadblocks. Chunks of concrete, old air conditioners, twisted car parts stood in the way of the Humvees as snipers and other gunmen aimed for the Americans. Sgt. Yihjyh Chen was a gunner whose job was to lead the convoy and clear the roads of danger. He was the first American to fall in the battle. The ambush was in full swing.

The soldiers who started the mission to help Sadr's citizens were pinned down and called for quick-response teams to help. Justin's group was supposed to roll, but they were unavailable. After returning from Palm Sunday Mass, where he was an altar server, Casey learned about the ambush: the killers on rooftops, the smoky killing zone. He volunteered to go. His sergeant asked him more than once, telling him that a mechanic did not have to put himself in this deadly situation. As was his nature, Casey stood firm. He would help. Cpl. Forest Jostes, who joined the service when he was seventeen and still in high school, rode in a truck behind Casey.

Justin's group was ready after Casey and Forest were already cornered in the killing zone. Justin loaded into his gunner's sling and set out to save Casey and Forest and the others who were pinned down by the rampaging mobs.

"Everybody became an infantryman that night," said Levi Lohnes, a soldier and a friend of Casey and Justin.

Justin's convoy maneuvered through gauntlets of burning tires. Terrorists aimed rocket-propelled grenades at him and his buddies. He was in a gunner's sling and had a 360-degree view of the pandemonium playing out in the streets. He watched guerillas blowing holes through his buddies' vehicles and smelled the fire and rancid stench of human waste. Aiming forward, feces

and urine splashed into his face. *The trucks were too close, man. They were sitting ducks with big targets on their backs.*

A shot blew through his Humvee and popped his tire.

Then a call came. Turn back. *Get out of there!*

Justin was trained to kill, even through fear that rattled every nerve. He needed to help. He couldn't leave buddies out there to die. His instinct was to do a Rambo, run toward the fire with guns blazing. Instead, he was the good soldier and followed orders to get out.

☆ ☆

CASEY'S GROUP didn't have a chance. They were cornered. Ambushed.

Casey's mother later said that he was able to shoot his weapon after the terrorists hit him. She also said that friendly fire might have killed Casey, but no official documents or reports say anything about that.

Forest Jostes died alongside Casey.

"From what we learned later, the first team made it through; my son was in the second team," recounted Diane Ibbotson, Forest's mother.[3] "There were four men in his group. Enemy fire wounded two men; the third member of the team assisted one of the wounded. My son, the fourth team member, was wounded and died while engaged in battle with the enemy."

Justin couldn't call home to his mother to tell her about the nightmare that took his friends. The lines were down for a few days to give the army time to contact the families of the men who died. When Justin finally made contact, he told his mother he was scared and tired.

"He said take the scariest ride you can think of, multiply it

about a million times, and that doesn't come close to what we are feeling here," Jan said.

Justin sent a letter to his fiancée, Shannon, on April 8, 2004, talking about the killing zone:

> A big battle broke out and we were in the middle of it. We had to escort wounded soldiers to another base and we were getting shot at. My front right tire got shot out . . . after our tire got fixed and on the way back to base, we got ambushed. They missed my truck but hit the one behind me. That night we lost 10 soldiers and 49 got wounded. I knew two of the ones that died. The next night we took a wrong turn and ended up in the middle of Sadr City around midnight. We had to drive through burning roadblocks, ram cars to get them out of our way and do about 60 mph to get out alive. We were informed that it is no longer a peacekeeping mission, it is war again! You could never know what it is like unless you are here. The feeling you get when 10 bullets zip by your head. It is a feeling like no other! OK, I know you don't want to know all that stuff because it makes you worry. I just wanted to let you know that I was OK.

LUKE HERBST roomed with Justin in Iraq. He also knew Casey, whose death shook the soldiers new in Iraq. They had jobs and they kept performing. But the last image Luke had of Casey was his bloody helmet in the back of a truck.

Luke called his mom and described the battles he fought and how he was scared and how he was praying and keeping right with God. Like a preacher talking about Satan himself, Luke described Sadr's army and Casey's killers as evil.

"They are evil. They are evil." He said it over and over again.

"I will never, ever forget Luke's voice and how scared he sounded," said Annette Meyer, Luke's mom. "I read this somewhere, 'If you haven't heard the shaking voice of a family member under war circumstances, you haven't heard real terror.'"

Two days after Casey died, Luke sent an e-mail home:

Hello everyone. Hope things are going good back in the States. Things here are heating up. In the last two days we have taken attacks. I've been fired at twice, one round hit the tire of the truck I was on and blew it out. Thank God we have run flats, so we were able to continue the mission.

I just got off of a mission, we were doing a route recon through Sadr City. They were burning tires and made walls of fire to block us from coming. We drove through the flames. Also their sewage systems run down the street and pools up in low spots. I got sprayed when our trucks went through it. I was covered in human waste. My goggles were covered so I couldn't see anything for two minutes, finally I got some water to clean them off. The only way I can really describe the feeling here is if you take all the haunted houses, roller coasters, scary movies, car wrecks you been in, and put them together and speed it up 1,000 times. If you haven't heard from CNN we lost 10 soldiers yesterday, and one was a buddy of mine. I worked with him [Casey Sheehan].

I'm sorry if this letter is a little down, I hope it doesn't scare you. But I didn't want to sugarcoat it. I'm doing good spiritually, mentally and physically. Just keep praying for me and the troops. In the last two days I have seen, smelled and tasted things I pray and hope no one will ever experience.

Just know this, I love all of you. Don't worry. Trust in the Lord, as I do. What else can I do? And keep praying. I'm glad to be here, despite all the horror that is here. I feel God put me here for a reason.

Well, I have to rack out, tired! Take care and here is a verse that I hold close to me.

Joel 3:9–10 [NKJV]

Proclaim this among the nations:

"Prepare for war!

Wake up the mighty men,

Let all the men of war draw near,

Let them come up.

Beat your plowshares into swords

And your pruninghooks into spears;

Let the weak say, "I am strong."

THE U.S. Department of Defense issued a press release about the deaths on April 4, 2004, Black Sunday. It confirmed eight deaths, not the ten that soldiers had heard about in early reports.

The Department of Defense announced today the death of eight soldiers supporting Operation Iraqi Freedom. They died on April 4, in Baghdad, Iraq, when their units were attacked with rocket-propelled grenades and small arms fire. Eight soldiers were assigned to two units at Fort Hood, Texas, while one soldier was assigned in Germany. Killed were:

Sgt. Michael W. Mitchell, 25, of Porterville, Calif., from the Army's 2nd Battalion, 37th Armor Regiment, 1st Brigade, 1st Armored Division, Ray Barracks, Friedberg, Germany.

Soldiers killed from the Army's 2nd Battalion, 5th Cavalry Regiment, 1st Cavalry Division, Fort Hood, Texas were:

Sgt. Yihjyh L. Chen, 31, of Saipan, Marianas Protectorate.

Spc. Robert R. Arsiaga, 25, of San Antonio, Texas.

Spc. Stephen D. Hiller, 25, of Opelika, Ala.

Spc. Ahmed A. Cason, 24, of McCalla, Ala.

Spc. Israel Garza, 25, of Lubbock, Texas.

Soldiers killed from the Army's 1st Battalion, 82nd Field Artillery Regiment, 1st Cavalry Division, Fort Hood, Texas were:

Cpl. Forest J. Jostes, 22, of Albion, Ill.

Spc. Casey Sheehan, 24, of Vacaville, Calif.

The incident is under investigation.[4]

SOLDIERS IN Iraq get precious time on computers or telephones to communicate with loved ones back home. Justin used some of that time to write condolences to the Sheehan family on a popular Web site honoring fallen soldiers, http://www.fallenheroesmemorial.com.

My name is Spc. Justin Johnson of the 1-82 field arty battalion. Casey was a great friend of mine and is missed by us. All I wanted to say he is in my heart all the time.

Jan believes that the post may have been the last thing Justin ever wrote.

6

DAY SIX

★ ★

They are spineless cowards. They don't fight like men—they
don't look you in the eye.

> —*Jan Johnson on the terrorists who*
> *killed her son*

JUSTIN WAS RUNNING ON anger and fear, a concoction that is sickening and necessary in war. Buddies were dead. It wasn't like the first days in Iraq when he drove toward Baghdad, standing in his turret, viewing the surroundings as if it were prom night and he was gazing out of a limousine sunroof. Things were different now. He wasn't so damned ignorant. Within days on the ground, he had fought in an all-out war. Insurgents, terrorists, and crazed kids made sport of taking out soldiers. Justin's head, bobbling around outside of his Humvee, was a fine target for a rocket-propelled grenade or a wild shot.

Inside his barracks, Justin wrote letters, talked about Casey, and read his Bible. He still liked joking around with the other guys. The living quarters weren't too shoddy—they were decent compared to tent cities where other troops were quartered.

Justin's platoon lived in an old secret police headquarters, so the three-person rooms had electricity. Justin's room was next door to the MWR (morale, welfare, and recreation), which had a large-screen television, foosball, pool tables, and a shop with snacks. Another TV room had satellite access.

"There also was an indoor swimming pool across from our barracks. So I have no qualms with the place except for it being in hell," said Keith Nimlo, one of Justin's closest friends. Justin called him "Old Man" because Keith was almost thirty years old. He had been in the service before. After September 11, when he watched the World Trade Center buildings burn and collapse, Keith marched into a recruiting office in New York City and signed up again.

Soldiers do what they can to distract themselves from the reality outside of the "wire" (meaning their base of operation, their security zone), where every inch or movement could be the last. Handheld games and even Nintendos for TV are helpful, but the realities of war weigh on them like a wet horse blanket. Every hour that a soldier stays up playing poker or billiards is another hour without sleep that a guy would beg for on another day. A guy has to sharpen his reflexes by plenty of rest. Booze isn't a problem in Iraq because of its Muslim persuasion. Americans can't have a sip of beer anymore than a suicide bomber who has sworn his life to Allah.

Even before they arrived in Iraq, Justin, Casey and their buddies talked about the war, how they would do in "the sandbox," and if they would make it home. Justin and his army "brother" Luke Herbst talked about deep issues. Life and death. They met in Fort Hood and bonded, as men will do, and loved each other like brothers. Luke and Justin had a lot in common. They liked to party and loved their families and God.

"I would have to say that the best thing that I ever did with Justin was the whole last month before we deployed. We really didn't do a whole lot but sit around drink beer, dip Skoal mint tobacco, and watch movies. We also would talk about what we thought the war would be like, if any of us would not be coming back, or someone getting really hurt and losing a leg. Just the stuff that comes to your mind. We talked about everything and anything to help calm our nerves for what we had to face in the year to come," Luke said.

ON APRIL 10, 2004, Sadr's army and Muslim rebels continued their attack on the coalition forces. Sadr City reeked of blood and human waste and burning rubber. Nothing unusual, except the overpowering smell of iron from human blood was sharper than usual. The smell blended with the normal stench permeating Sadr City from rotting piles of vegetables, roaming billy goats, and bags of household trash baked in the hot sun. Skeletons of burned-out Humvees lay where soldiers had abandoned them in firefights. Before leaving trucks behind during the heat of war, soldiers stripped them of anything that the enemy could later use against them, such as radio codes, weapons, and other items.

Keith went out on a run to face the enemy in the burning slum. As he maneuvered with his guys through the filth, a roadside bomb hit his vehicle. He had been through this before a couple times, and luck left him alive with only burns to his legs.

"You just hope that you see it before it explodes," Keith said of the IEDs (improvised explosive devices). "It's a roll of the dice."

This time the concussion of the explosion cracked his windshield and deafened him.

"I had ringing in my ears and they were bleeding," Keith said. He was taken to an aid station then released to go back to his barracks. Justin was hanging out there and ready to give Keith a hard time about the IED. Laughing your way through war is better than crying.

"What happened old man?" Justin asked.

Keith told him about the hell outside of the wire and the bombs and his bleeding ears.

"He told me 'You better keep your head down, old man.'"

They both laughed.

As Keith slept that night, Justin and his crew readied for combat. Fear had to be pushed aside so he could function. A gunner has to keep his wits about him. Darkness settled in around him and the others as they moved toward the gauntlet of death where Casey Sheehan had died six days earlier. The smell of death seized the air around them, but there was no flinching now.

Justin manned his high-powered gun from the turret as he searched the road in front of him and to the sides for anything that could kill him or others. Terrorists stuffed garbage, animal carcasses, and decaying human bodies with bombs. Then they waited for a target to align with the booby-trapped roadside trap. The terrorists used cell phones to trigger the bombs. Even remote-control toy trucks helped America's enemies kill troops, carrying bombs beneath passing cars. The killers would sometimes wait and watch from a sand dune or move on to plant another bomb meant for another American.

Justin angled toward what soldiers called "IED Alley," a *Mad Max* run of crippled and blackened vehicles that made good hiding spots for homemade bombs.

"We must have found ninety-nine IEDs there since we were in Iraq," Keith said.

IEDs are the weapon of choice for the terrorists in Iraq because they are fairly easy to build, transport, and detonate. In addition to cell phones, they use washer-timers and garage-door openers to detonate the devices. The improvised bombs cause most combat deaths in the Iraq War, according to the Department of Defense.

The dark night offered little help for Justin as he surveyed the ground. His driver pointed a flashlight out of the Humvee with his left hand as he controlled the truck with his right hand. Then a deep thump shook them like King Kong rattling a hamster cage.

Soldiers fight the reflex to flee when a buddy is down. Sometimes they're not sure who is hit or if they might die themselves. The shock of concussion overwhelms the pain—at least for a split second. Troops may stagger through their jobs with a fatal blow to their bodies.

"It's the gunner! Johnson!"

"Our gunner's hit!"

"Sergeant . . . it's JJ!"

Justin was declared dead at 11:45 p.m., Iraqi time.

Keith was in his barracks, stealing a wink after his run-in with the IED. "I remember clear as day when they came and told me," Keith said.

Keith had to collect some personnel information on Justin so army officials could find Jan and Joe and notify them. He delivered the stuff and then was ordered back outside the wire. No time for crying. His soul was screaming, and the sky was still black with night and war.

"I don't think I was ever so scared in my life," he said.

"Justin was gone."

Crews towed Justin's Humvee back to base. Its tires were flat, and Justin's turret was splashed with his blood. Nobody bothered to clean it out before the next crew of Justin's friends took the Humvee out a few days later for another run.

WORD SPREADS fast inside the wire when a soldier falls. Levi made peace with himself by writing about what he saw or knew about the war. Some of his blogs were published in *People* magazine. This is what he wrote about Justin's last stand:

> I was interrupted the other night while typing this. A nervous specialist running the internet café rushed into the room, his squeaky voice breaking the soft sounds of keyboard clicking, telling us that communications were to be cut off immediately due to an attack that had taken casualties moments prior. The next day I found out that those casualties were friends from my platoon. One almost lost his arm, and the other unfortunately did not make it.
>
> I remember hanging out in Austin with Z [a friend who almost lost his arm] the week before we deployed. It was an uneasy night. Z, our other friend, and I were nursing beers in the corner patio at Club Deville, one of Austin's many "swank" bars. We felt cut off from the carefree life happening around us. Z kept nervously shuffling around, saying he didn't have a good feeling about Iraq; he was clearly troubled by his prophetic thoughts. Our other friend and I tried to tell him he couldn't think like that, that things would be all right. It was impossible not to think about where we'd be a month from that point in time. Feeling awkward and detached from the inebriated atmos-

phere of civilian glee, we called it a night earlier than usual. This party didn't belong to us anymore.

Z's and Justin's fate was sealed by an IED now a little over a month later. Out of respect for individuals and families, I don't mention names of the wounded or dead without approval.

It's hard to describe this feeling of subtraction. The loss of a friend or acquaintance floods the mind with every single memory you have of them. All of them newly minted as profound moments. Our trip to Mexico, the $10 buckets of beer we binged on at the Black Cat Bar in Matamoros, the senoritas we met, our buzzed conversations about the beauty of this world while we lounged on body boards in the salt-stained waters of the Gulf as the sun swam into the ocean. I prefer to remember the sun setting in this ocean. It's a piece of heaven in my mind and Justin Johnson is there.

No action can be taken to absolve this. Revenge is only a reaction that fades in me. Of course I want those responsible for this to suffer our wrath, but my priority right now is to protect and preserve what isn't for the taking, and assist in the capture or killing (if need be) of those that are responsible for the aggression against us and the good people of Sadr City.

We are bruised with the losses endured but not in poor spirits. I think we'd dishonor the memory of our friends by doing so. I know in my platoon we still laugh, we still joke, and we still berate each other like we did in Fort Hood. We make it as "normal" as can be. I can say we're a little dumbfounded that all of this has taken place and it's only our second week! Anyone could foresee the possibility of this happening but none figured it would be this intense so soon.[1]

SOULS ON FIRE

I guess my main reason over here is for revenge—not just for
Justin but for September 11, for the USS *Cole.*
—*Joe Johnson*

The person who killed my son, I have no animosity for that
person at all.
—*Cindy Sheehan, August 16, 2005,*
media conference

My Baby, My Son, My Soldier
Born on a bright morn in the month of June
Into a little man he would grow too soon.
From there to a bright teen, full of class,
Ready to take on the world and kick some ass.
U.S. Army was to be his career of choice
Over this I did not rejoice.
When we found out soon he would be Iraq bound,
My heart just slowly hit the ground.
He was excited, ready to roll,
Thinking he was ready for his first patrol.
Twelve days later he was gone for good,
No longer to see Texas or good ole' Fort Hood.
Instead my boy came home to me one night,
After he had made one very long flight.
Gone was the man we thought he would be,
It was my baby they returned to me.
—*Jan Johnson, 2005*

THE JOHNSONS WERE NUMB. There was no other way to function. The part of the brain that allows a person to see reality has to shut down enough to survive the shock and sawing pain of a child's death. Grief in its first stages can allow a mother to smile at visitors and even pick out her baby's casket. Sometimes the numbness isn't enough to stop the nightmares that come in the day. These nightmares prick at the consciousness and scream at the heart, "I'm dead, Mom. Dead."

Jan waited for Joe to make it home to Georgia from Washington. There was no sleep for her, just a fuzzy place between wide-awake and wishing to die. In the meantime, Joe had help from a soldiers' emergency fund so he could attend Justin's funeral.

Justin's body went to Dover Air Force Base, Delaware, before its journey to Atlanta and then finally home to Rome. Jan and Joe did not drive to Atlanta to meet their son's remains. They felt it would be better to be able to view Justin privately rather than collect a closed casket at the busy Atlanta airport. So they waited for the funeral home and the army to bring him home.

Night set on Rome as the Johnsons waited for their boy. About 9:00 p.m. the hearse pulled in to Henderson and Sons Funeral Home. Men opened the rear of the vehicle and gently slid out a large white cardboard box that protected a military-issue casket. Inside was Justin.

A good friend, Eddie McSwain, showed up before Jan and Joe, who arrived at the funeral home about ten minutes or so after the hearse. Jan's grief and fear shook her until the numbness—which was becoming a constant companion—allowed her to process what was going on. *This is your baby boy. He's home now. He's home.* Joe stood quietly until Jan broke down. Her shoulders shook with each sob.

The army assistance officer went into a viewing room and

adjusted Justin's medals, straightened his uniform, and made sure everything was okay for Joe and Jan. Justin's body had been prepared by mortuary specialists at the Dover base. Jan turned to Joe, who did not want an open casket, and told her husband that he did not have to look at Justin. She would go by herself. She just had to see if this nightmare was real.

"I've got to see for myself," she said. "I know they took fingerprints, but I don't care."

When it was time to see her boy, Jan reached for Joe's hand, and they walked together into the viewing room. Jan's eyes moved slowly over her son's body and her heart broke again. She saw stitches around his hairline, but she never found out why they were there. Justin wore white gloves. *Why? Why the gloves? Did he lose his hand or did shrapnel cut him so bad? What happened to my baby?* Jan wanted to hold him and kiss him and love him. She wanted to make it better for everyone. For Justin. That's what a mother does.

Jan and Joe hoped to bury Justin at Myrtle Hill Cemetery, which has a lot of history that reaches back beyond the Civil War. The cemetery sits on one of Rome's seven hills—all of which are named after the seven hills of the ancient city of Rome. If you stand near a Confederate memorial here, you can see for miles. At least, that's what it feels like. Looking northeast, you get a good look at the town of Rome. Going east, the Etowah Valley fills your view. The southern view points you to the Appalachian foothills. On a quiet night, the souls of the cemetery sing. So much heartache, so much life.

Almost a hundred years before any Civil War soldiers were laid to rest in Myrtle, "General John Sevier descended upon Cherokee, Georgia, from Tennessee chasing Indians who had scalped and killed thirteen people at Cavett's Station near

Knoxville."[1] Sevier, a future governor of the Volunteer State, chased the tribesmen to Myrtle Hill, where they fought. About 120 Cherokees perished on the site. Later, after the Trail of Tears, in which the U.S. government forced Cherokees off their native lands into encampments, the cemetery at Myrtle was born.

The Confederate section of Myrtle is the final resting place of 377 soldiers from both sides of the Civil War. Their graves line the base of the hill near the entrance. Monuments tower over the cemetery and mark the proud heritage of the Confederacy. The United Daughters of the Confederacy erected a monument in memory of Gen. Nathan Bedford Forrest for his valor while fighting off Yankee marauders from a siege of the city.

A southwest section of the cemetery was set aside for blacks in a time when blacks and whites were buried in separate areas of the graveyard.

Visitors to Rome stop at Myrtle Hill for a taste of Southern history. President Woodrow Wilson's first wife, Ellen Axson Wilson, was a native of Rome and is buried here. She is the only first lady buried in Georgia.

During World War I, Floyd County lost thirty-four men. The city planted thirty-four magnolia trees to honor each of the fallen. Today, the trees are grand and strong with deep roots.

For Jan and Joe, their son belonged to the people of Floyd County. He should lie among others who fought for America. After all, Justin was the first soldier from the county to die in the Iraq War. He was history.

Buying a gravesite at Myrtle Hill is no small feat due to the hill's historical significance and the scarcity of available graves. As they faced the reality of Justin's death, mourning with each

breath, Jan and Joe had to appeal to the city council for permission to bury their son. The council had to consider the significance of Justin's life and death to the city. The mortuary handled the details, and the council agreed that Justin should lie among Rome's other heroes.

"We wanted him there because of the history," Jan said. "When we said something about it to the funeral director, we really didn't think it would happen."

The night before the services, the family held a visitation at the North Rome Church of God. Jan looked at Justin so many times. She still couldn't understand why he wore gloves. At one point she wanted to reach for his hand to see if it was there, but Josh stopped her.

Emotions were toppling over. When Joe and Jan's daughter, Joleen, who was pregnant with her second child, heard that Justin was dead, she went into labor. It was too early to have the baby, and doctors stopped the contractions.

"The morning of visitation, I went into labor again. And I went up there [to the hospital]. I said, 'Stop it. The visitation's tonight, funeral tomorrow. Just stop it. You can take it Sunday—take the baby Sunday. I don't care. But just stop it right now.' So they stopped it."

The visitation was surreal, as if the Johnsons were sitting at somebody else's wake. But there was Justin. The sight of him stretched out in the casket snapped them out of the haze like a gunshot to the gut. Despite the solemn situation and the overwhelming grief, a woman the Johnsons didn't know approached Jan and began talking to her about how George Bush was to blame for Justin's death. This woman said she too had lost a son. She understood Jan's grief. Wouldn't Jan join her in opposing Bush? The Johnsons could hardly believe that somebody would

come to them in their worst moments and politicize their son's death. They turned the woman away.

On April 17, 2004, the services for Justin overwhelmed not only the Johnsons but also the town. This was their boy. Hundreds showed up out of respect for their fallen brother and hero. The route from the North Rome Church of God to Myrtle Hill was painted in red, white, and blue. Brand-new police motorcycles took to the road for the very first time during Justin's procession. The flags at the old courthouse on Tribune Street flew at half-staff.

The stress got to Joleen. As the family prepared to go to the graveyard, the contractions started again.

"I made it all the way through the funeral at the church," she said. "And they got down to the graveyard and I was just hurtin'. They were like three minutes apart then. And there were some paramedics down there and they said, 'We need to take you on to the emergency room.' And I said, 'No, I'm fine. I'm fine. I'm fine.'"

After the funeral, Joleen went to the hospital for another shot. A week later, she gave birth to a five-pound girl. She named her Justine.

Jan lived in a blur on the day of the funeral. But at least she lived. She does have one image that sticks out. As she rode to Myrtle Hill in the procession down Broad Street, she looked out of the limousine and saw all of the people waving flags. Young and old, strangers and neighbors. A World War II veteran hanging on to a walker came into focus. As the hearse passed, he took his hand off of the walker and saluted.

VACAVILLE MAYOR Len Augustine received the call that a young man from his town had been killed in Iraq. The town had been

through this once already. It seemed too soon to mourn another of its sons. The mayor took it personally and wore the grief as if his own boys died in the sand of a foreign land.

As a Vietnam veteran and retired air force officer, Mayor Augustine had felt war. Tasted it. Smelled it. Thank God, he survived it. Memories of 'Nam are tattooed like a sailor's blue anchor on his mind.

The day he went to visit the Sheehan family to hold them and cry with them, the sounds and fears and pain and strength came back to him.

He had been a captain in the air force. He had the honor— the raw pain—of escorting an airman's body to New Jersey. Back to the family. To a hero's grave when so many lost in Vietnam were treated as criminals when they returned home.

Now, even two years after Casey's death, Mayor Augustine notes every detail of the Sheehans' mourning and compares the gaping loss to that of the airman's family decades ago. He sat down at the Perfect Blend Coffee House in Vacaville to recount this time in a low, respectful, even tone. Like a poet reciting a sad sonnet. The mayor is a strong man with sharp shoulders and soft eyes that tell stories all by themselves.

"I remember very vividly the effect on that family," the mayor recalled. As he spoke about the journey, remembering, his baby blue eyes moistened. He looked around at the citizens of his town who had stopped for a game of checkers and some conversation at the coffeehouse. Refocusing on the table in front of him, he said, "I saw that same awful pain in the Sheehans."

Vacaville's people, strangers and all, stopped by the Sheehans with flowers, cards, and even offerings of money. The city mourned with the family.

"I take it personally when something happens to one of

us," Augustine said. "The whole city really acts like a family in these times. It was painful."

Augustine wears the pain like a seasoned warrior who understands the humanity of his enemies. He is humbled by his time in the air force in which he was at one time responsible for organizing the transportation of President Ronald Reagan and his wife, Nancy. He retired from Travis Air Force Base and fell in love with Vacaville. When he had his chance, he ran for mayor. Augustine and Vacaville vice mayor Pauline Clancy are known as the air base's strongest advocates.

Led by Augustine and Clancy, the city council voted unanimously to name April 13, 2004, "Casey Austin Sheehan Memorial Day." All flags in the city were lowered to half-mast and the council issued a proclamation:

> Greetings! To all who pass this way through our beloved City of Vacaville, a Place of Peace, let it be known far and wide that one of our own brightest, faithful and most courageous young men, United States Army Specialist Casey Austin Sheehan, made the ultimate sacrifice in the service of his country while volunteering to fight in the War on Terrorism in Iraq.
>
> It is with deep respect and sympathy that we remember Casey as a role model for the thousands of dedicated military men and women who daily face the rigors and danger of war without hesitation or regret. Casey Sheehan was more than a soldier; he was a son, a brother, a grandchild, a friend, a neighbor, a student, an Eagle Scout, and an altar server in his church; he was a patriot, a volunteer, a leader who stepped out front, taking on responsibility and putting himself in harm's way rather than having others do so.
>
> He knew the risks; he could have come home, but he chose

to reenlist and he did so because of his belief in what he was doing. He loved his country and his God and he felt secure in those beliefs. Casey Austin Sheehan is an American hero. Our community mourns his passing and we will always be thankful to him and his family for his loyal service and his very special life.

Therefore, we, the mayor and City Council of the City of Vacaville, on behalf of a grateful and caring community, do hereby declare today, Tuesday, April 13, 2004, as Casey Austin Sheehan Memorial Day.

CINDY AND Pat made arrangements with the Nadeau Family Funeral Home to handle the Mass. Steve Nadeau is a lifelong Catholic, parishioner at St. Mary's Catholic Church, and a friend to the Sheehans. He would take care of their son's remains and ensure that Casey was honored as a loyal Catholic and patriotic American.

Forced to live the life of mourning, the Sheehans huddled together and tried to make the hard decisions, such as choosing Casey's grave site and his last outfit. They had always done everything as one, and now one of them was gone. Families suffering from a sudden death see glimpses of themselves as they mourn. They can still laugh together when their guts feel like screaming. The Sheehans watched old *Saturday Night Live* episodes to jerk them out of their bubbles of fear. It was a distraction that couldn't save them from the emotions that tore them into tiny pieces of anger, depression, and ultimately, raw reality. Like seeing Casey's body for the first time.

The Sheehans wanted to meet Casey's body at the airport, so Nadeau arranged for a stretch limousine. His hearse and the

limo arrived at San Francisco International Airport. Two soldiers greeted the family. They removed a long cardboard box that protected Casey's hardwood casket during its transport. Casey's siblings wept as the casket was moved into the hearse. The soldiers also wept.

Two years after the trip to the airport, Cindy accused the army of mishandling Casey's remains. Her accusations came as she deflected widespread criticisms that she had not yet placed a headstone on Casey's grave. *Vanity Fair* magazine ran a photo of Cindy lying across Casey's grave. It had no headstone. Cindy answered her critics in a piece for Berkeley-based blog *Truthout:*

> I will tell the world why Casey has no marker yet. In the first place, does anyone who is attacking me know how Casey was brought home from Iraq? We picked him up in the United loading dock in a cardboard box and he was off-loaded into a hearse without one honor guard. We had to wait for about a half-hour on a curb near the United freight area for his one escort, who rode from Dover Air Force Base in a seat, while Casey was treated as an over-sized piece of luggage. Has anybody held her other sobbing children who are sitting on a curb in San Francisco, waiting for the remains of their big brother to be carried over to the dock by a forklift?[2]

The pain and shock of seeing Casey's casket burned. Their souls were on fire.

"The most heartbreaking aspect of seeing Casey lying in his casket for me was that his face was flat again because he had no muscle tone. He looked like he did when he was a baby lying in his bassinet," Cindy wrote.[3]

St. Mary's Church was warm inside on the spring day that

mourners said good-bye to Casey Sheehan. Parishioners, local dignitaries, city residents, and veterans from other wars sat shoulder to shoulder in pews as the priests performed the rituals releasing Casey's soul to his Father in heaven. Members of the Knights of Columbus served at the Mass in full regalia: a cape highlighted in deep purple with a matching helmet topped by purple feathers. Pat was a member of the Knights, the world's largest Catholic family fraternal organization whose holy purpose is to defend family, country, and church. The group's roots stretch back to the 1800s, and its name comes from Christopher Columbus.

Cindy wore a light green skirt and jacket. Her face was pale like a woman who had cried her life away. Pat dressed in a dark suit. He wore a red, white, and blue ribbon on his jacket above his heart. Throughout the Mass, Cindy leaned on her husband for support and sometimes reached for her surviving son, Andy. She also wore the red, white, and blue ribbon, but on her right side.

After the Mass, after Casey received the blessing of the promised resurrection, a procession led him through town and to the Vacaville-Elmira Cemetery where former mayors and veterans and cowboys and airmen lie. Casey's grave was open, and his casket sat above it, seemingly floating between heaven and earth. Mourners sang. The priest offered more blessings.

Before the casket was lowered into its early grave, Casey's little brother lowered his head to the casket and sweetly kissed his brother good-bye.

THE MINISTERS

The kids are very appreciative of everything we give them,
the candy, the school supplies. And that is another reason
why I'm here, for the kids.

—Joe Johnson on building
infrastructure in Iraq

I was a Catholic youth minister for eight years. Now being a
peace activist is my full-time job.

—Cindy Sheehan[1]

THE CHURCH WAS SUPPOSED to help heal the pain of loss.
Christians know the story of Jesus and Lazarus and how
Jesus broke down when his friend died. He couldn't bear the
grief, so he raised him from the dead. Where was God now?
That's what Joe wanted to know.

Joe and the family had served God. They had all gone down
to Armuchee Creek, and the preacher baptized them in the cold
water. They went to church and prayed. Sure, Joe cussed every
now and then, and he used to drink plenty, but that was no rea-
son for this punishment.

"I was furious at God," Joe said.

Joe and God had a good relationship before Justin was
killed. Joe still loved God, that goes without saying. He loved
God so much that, even as he prepared to bury his boy, he and

Jan asked the preacher to have an altar call. Ministers use altar calls as opportunities for individuals to respond to the gospel message recently proclaimed to them. They ask folks to raise their hands or approach the altar as a visible profession of faith. About ten people, some of them elderly, raised their hands at Justin's funeral during the altar call.

☆ ☆

THE NORTH Rome Church of God sends missionaries around the world to aid the less fortunate, people who live in dirt or open homes that are vulnerable to Mother Nature's wrath. When Jan's friend invited her to a brotherhood breakfast, some of the church's missionaries showed slides of mission trips. Later the church held its yearly mission's banquet, with loads of more enticing pictures. The photos of the environments and the people appealed to Jan's heart and sense of adventure. She was no girly girl. She liked the idea of traveling to places where the people had no clue about freeway congestion, towering buildings, or even indoor plumbing.

"I'd go wander around and find myself back at the Ecuador displays," she said.

Jan had plenty of skills to help the helpless. Joe's father was a homebuilder who taught Joe the trade. Joe in turn passed the skills on to Jan and all of his kids, including his daughter Joleen, who is no bigger than one leg of an average journeyman carpenter. Jan learned to bang on roof shingles, pour a house foundation, install windows, and set kitchen cabinets. The family had started a business called J&J Construction, which they later changed to Johnson Construction.

Church leaders told the Johnsons they could use their skills on that mission to Ecuador, but Joe and Jan would have to raise

the money to get themselves to South America. Like a miracle of sunshine's arm reaching down through thick, gray clouds, the money came to them through friends. Their mission trip lasted from mid-September through November 2001.

Before leaving for Ecuador, Joe and Jan left a list of things to do in case they died. They wrote contact numbers of relatives who would need to know and listed their wishes for burial. Joe had wanted to be an organ donor, but that might be difficult in a third-world country that doesn't have antibiotics on a regular basis. Their three kids were old enough to care for themselves while they remodeled a church and built a pulpit for the Church of God in Ecuador. While they were there, they decided to be baptized a second time. A preacher took Joe and Jan to a river whose water was as cold as a melting iceberg and baptized them into the Church of God.

As the time stretched further away from the day Justin died, Jan thought her husband might settle down. Maybe he would forget about going to Iraq. Then something would rev him up. A news story. Somebody asking about Justin. Jan knew she couldn't convince Joe to stay home.

"I knew he would never heal if he didn't go," she said.

Jan's heart had a glimpse of peace when Joe decided against deploying with Georgia's Forty-eighth Brigade Combat Team. Joe had been activated with the Forty-eighth in December, ten months after Justin died. But by February, she knew she couldn't handle Joe leaving her. Her heart was too raw. Joe just couldn't abandon her. The National Guard allowed him to stay home because the family had lost Justin.

The decision ate at Joe. He wasn't a quitter, and the thought of revenge electrified him, shooting through his nerves like gas through an engine. He could not keep the thoughts away. *Justin*

. . . Killers . . . Hate . . . I hate them . . . My boy . . . Oh, God . . . Justin . . .

"I think about my unit every day," Joe told his hometown newspaper.[2] "I know I need to be home for my wife right now, but I feel like I've let the guys down."

Almost one year to the day that Justin died in Sadr City, Joe called his unit in Georgia and said that he was anxious to get to Iraq. The armed forces have their own schedule and aren't necessarily concerned with a father's plans to avenge his son's death. It doesn't matter that the son was killed while on duty and that his father is a seasoned soldier raring to go into combat. The guys in charge will decide when they're ready for another warrior. Not before.

"The day I heard that Justin had been killed, I vowed to him and God that if given the chance to come here, I would kill as many as I possibly could. I reckon I can live with the fact that I may not accomplish that," Joe said.

Joe waited for the call to go, but he heard nothing for almost three months.

"I told them, 'Hey, I'm ready to go,'" Joe said. "When I didn't hear anything from them, I guessed they thought I was a little too psycho."

As the days passed, his anxiety and hate festered. The love and compassion he felt as a Christian missionary dimmed under the darkness of rage. He hated Muslims. He wanted to kill them.

Slaughter them for Justin. For September 11 . . . Just kill them . . . Stop the pain.

God didn't help him with the swirl of bitterness that burned inside. Joe had worked for God. He built homes for the poor. He did it for God. How could God turn on him like this?

☆ ☆

SEVEN MONTHS after Justin died, Joe was antsy but took time before Thanksgiving to speak with CNN about his wish to fight in Iraq. He and Jan met with Heidi Collins, a veteran news reporter in an interview that aired on November 15, 2004.

COLLINS: Good morning to both of you. Thanks for being here once again, you guys.

JAN: Good morning.

JOE: Good morning.

COLLINS: I want to ask you first and foremost, as we have said, it's only been seven months since you lost Justin. How are you feeling today?

JOE: Angry. Very mad at the terrorists. I really don't know much to say other than that. I feel like we're still doing the right thing over there. And we don't want the boys to come home yet, because if they do, we feel like that they would have died for nothing. They need to stay and get the job done.

COLLINS: Mr. Johnson, you mentioned anger and that the guys are doing the right thing over there. Is that why you're going back?

JOE: Yes ma'am. I'm actually looking forward to being in Iraq, but I'm not looking forward to leaving my family and all of the training before we go. But as far as actually getting in country, I'm looking forward to it.

COLLINS: In fact, you will quite possibly be putting your life on the line, just as your son did.

JOE: Yes ma'am.

COLLINS: What are the thoughts that go through your mind when you think about that?

JOE: Yes. Well, I really don't think about it right now. We had

some other people ask us the other day if I was nervous or scared. And I said, no, not right now, but I'm sure the time will come.

COLLINS: Mrs. Johnson, I imagine you are feeling an array of emotions right now. As you consider this next phase, if you will, what are your thoughts?

JAN: Well, I'm proud that my husband feels the way he does, as far as wanting to go and serve his country, even at his age. But at the same time, I don't want him going, because we've got grandchildren that I would like to know that they're going to see him when he—you know, as they grow up.

COLLINS: In fact, I know you have . . .

JAN: And while he's gone.

COLLINS: That's right. I know you have a young granddaughter, who was actually named after your son, Justin. Some people would say, Mr. Johnson, that your family has sacrificed enough. What do you say to them?

JOE: Well, they're probably right. But I've wanted to do this for a long time, as far as being able to do something for my country. And I found out a year and a half ago that I was still young enough to come back in. And so I jumped on it, hoping to get deployed.

COLLINS: It's been twenty-two years that you've been out of the military.

JOE: Yes ma'am.

COLLINS: What is your greatest concern as you go back now at this age?

JOE: Right now, hurting my knee again. I got hurt in training eight months ago or so—nine months ago. And my knee is still a little bit weak, but I hope to get it in shape before I actually get over there.

COLLINS: Well, again, it's wonderful talking to the both of you. We appreciate your time here this morning, and it gives us a lot to think about today as we watch some of the marines from Fallujah, we talk to a little bit later on, who tell us the same thing that you do. They want to go back. Something hard for some of us to understand.

☆ ☆

THE SOLDIERS of Joe's company had been in Iraq for almost four months before he would get there. He would be a replacement, taking over for a guy who either died, fell ill, or left Iraq for other extraordinary circumstances. Finding soldiers to take Joe's job isn't easy because most aren't Rambo types who enjoy heading a convoy with a big fat target on them. Joe is a rare breed of warrior who can survive on adrenaline as the world is burning down around him. He can steady his trigger finger and maintain focus on his target.

His missions to third-world countries helped prepare him for his work in Iraq. In Ecuador, Joe and Jan had learned to survive in rough neighborhoods where kids, called shoeshine boys, would kill you for a few coins. They also learned how to communicate with people of foreign cultures. Joe always connected with the children, a gift that would later be his salvation in Iraq.

The army called Joe in July 2005 and told him he would be leaving for Fort Drum, New York, in eight days. Then he would be sent to Iraq.

"I got off the phone with him and thought, 'He's getting his wish,'" Jan said.

After fits and starts, staying home for Jan and nursing a bad knee, Joe was finally on his way to the Iraqi slums where

terrorists had killed his son. He had a short stop at Fort Drum in New York for some training.

☆ ☆

FATHER MICHAEL MCFADDEN is a tall, strong-boned man with the milky skin of the Irish and blue eyes that can alternately radiate love and solemnity. He is pastor of Saint Mary's Catholic Church in Vacaville, a proud parish whose members include the town's mayor and families who built the city. McFadden knows what is happening in his church, whether petty gossip or impending death, and he's not one to fiddle around with either.

"Do you see that crucifix? It is the exact one used in the movie *Amadeus*," Father McFadden said as he motioned toward a wall with a lone cross. "Amadeus had a great gift, but sometimes a gift can become a burden."

The Roman Catholic priest loves his parish, which has a long history in Vacaville that includes fires, earthquakes, dismissed priests, family ties, and, most recently, Cindy Sheehan.

McFadden met Cindy when he transferred to St. Mary's in 2003. Cindy was the youth minister who organized events to help young people connect to the Catholic Church. The traditions of the church can sometimes intimidate newcomers. It's hard to understand men wearing long, flowing robes and burning incense if you were not reared around the rituals. Cindy was supposed to help, and by most accounts she did a fair job.

"Oh, Cindy was wonderful with the kids for so long," said Mary Ferrari, an old friend. "She took them on trips and helped them love the Lord. Really, Cindy was a wonderful, beautiful friend. She used to come into the church and kiss me on the forehead."

Cindy's best friend, Liz Kroman, helped her with the Catholic kids, planning events and teaching them the peaceful ways of Jesus.

"I was her sidekick," Liz said. "We had so much fun together, and the kids were always happy. It was very spiritual."

Before Father McFadden took over at Saint Mary's, the parish had gone through a couple priests. The church felt the growing pains of the city. Vacaville's population diversified in the past couple of decades as families from the San Francisco Bay Area moved northward for affordable housing, open space, and less crime. But the population shift brought murders, robberies, and economic complications with it. The changes echoed in the aisles of Saint Mary's. The transplants had a tinge of liberalism in their blood, and they were more likely to challenge traditional Catholic beliefs, such as the right to life. This didn't sit too well in Vacaville. The pastor juggled the factions in the church and sometimes was caught in the middle.

"Everywhere we see politics," Father McFadden said. "Schools, government—even the Church."

☆ ☆

BEFORE THE Sheehans moved to Vacaville in 1993, they regularly attended Mass in the Southern California city of Norwalk. The kids went to St. John of God Catholic School where folks mourned Casey's death years after he moved away.[3] When they packed up and moved north to Vacaville, the Sheehans brought their religion and strong Catholic fellowship with them.

Once they settled in a rented house in a newer neighborhood, the Sheehan family made a second home at Saint Mary's Catholic Church in Vacaville. The ancient ways of the Roman Catholic Church were etched in the family's souls. Catholicism

is natural to most Irishmen, like breathing air or a nip of good whiskey. They knew every prayer and each precise movement of the priest as he celebrated the body of Christ, calling down the two-thousand-year-old blessing that turns everyday bread into the body of their Savior. And Pat joined the Knights of Columbus.

When Casey became an altar server at eight years old,[4] he already knew where to stand during the priest's homily, how to pour water over the priest's hands for the cleansing before Communion; he had seen it a thousand times since his own baptism. The church's rituals intrigued Casey so much that some believed he might one day give his life to God and wear the vestments of a Roman Catholic priest.

Cindy knew her son wanted a different type of marriage.

"Even after he graduated from high school he stayed active in the ministry, helping me as a young-adult leader," she wrote. "He hoped one day to be a permanent deacon in the church. Deacons can get married and serve the church in various ways."

Cindy was a controversial minister. Sometimes she would show up at the church wearing shorts and a tank top and barefoot. It was as if she were trying to blend in with the teens of her youth group. Parents complained that Cindy's teachings were unorthodox and sometimes strayed far from Catholicism. Some of her students remember lessons on how to live the life of vegetarianism.

Membership in the youth group faded as the kids grew older. Cindy's group dwindled to the point that it included only her own children and maybe a couple of others. Meetings were held at Cindy's home instead of the church.

"The only time she came here was to collect her check," Father McFadden said.

Tension among factions in the church exploded. Cindy was the head of one faction and she had loyal friends. She and Father McFadden butted heads, and she began working to get him fired.

"You know the words Cindy used about the president?" McFadden asked. "I recognize those words. She called me a liar."

The stress of clashing with Cindy and her followers beat at McFadden's health. He was getting sick. In the past, he had been a heavy drinker, but he had given it up some years ago. Cindy and her crowd would have been a good excuse to tip the bottle again, but McFadden would not weaken. He stood up and did the right thing by his parish. He fired Cindy from her thirty-thousand-dollar-a-year position.

"It's a good thing I'm a stubborn Irishman," he said.

Cindy was not satisfied with McFadden's explanation for her dismissal, so she took it to a higher level. She contacted the Sacramento Diocese and sent e-mails to the bishops. When she became impatient with the diocese's answers, she fired off derogatory e-mails to the bishops, again using strong language not usually aimed at church leaders.

"I saw the e-mails, and she called Bishop Richard J. Garcia a liar," Father McFadden said.

He asked Cindy to come to the rectory so they could speak about their problems. "I told her that maybe we could work this out so she could come back to work," McFadden said. "She didn't want to."

Two years after he fired Cindy, the emotions surrounding the incident still gnaw at him. Discussing it tightens his jaw muscles. Scars still run through his parish, which continues to welcome the Sheehan family as their own.

When Casey died, McFadden did not officiate at the Mass.

A former parish priest did the honors. McFadden took a backseat to help the family heal. And he watched from St. Mary's as Cindy left Christianity and morphed into the world's most recognizable antiwar, anti-Bush activist.

Cindy drifted away from her old friends at church.

"She is not the Cindy I knew," Mary Ferrari said. "The person I knew wouldn't do these things—talk like that and curse. I enjoyed knowing Cindy Sheehan, but she is no longer my friend. I lost her."

When asked about Cindy, another old friend tossed up her hands and looked to heaven.

"She's in the hands of God," she said.

McFadden wants so much for his parish to heal, but constant media attention to Cindy's every move reopens the wounds.

"When all of this happened, I tried to stay away from the media," McFadden said. "I had satellite TV trucks out here. It was unbelievable."

Months after Casey died, Cindy severed her relationship with the Catholic Church and Christianity. She now refers to herself as a "recovering Catholic" while Pat and some of her children go to church regularly.

Every day, Mary prays for Cindy. "I pray that she comes to her senses," she said.

☆ ☆

ON FEBRUARY 29, 2006, three Girl Scouts from Troop 63 sold cookies in front of St. Mary's Church. Girl Scout cookies are a delicacy in these parts. Folks just can't wait to get their thin mints. Besides, girls in uniform are quite respectable in a military town. On this Sunday after four Masses, the parishioners

had an extra incentive to buy more than their annual supply of cookies. The Girl Scouts planned to send boxes—as many as people would buy—to American soldiers in Iraq. The girls ran out of cookies, leaving their leader, Alice Stone, scurrying for more.

"In all the years I have sold cookies, I have never seen them go so fast," Alice said. "Maybe they're sending a message. This used to be Cindy Sheehan's church."

JIHAD JOE

I knew it would hurt my wife and my family, but I had to go
to war.

—*Joe Johnson*

JOE ARRIVED AT FORT DRUM on August 2. He tried getting his
bearings so he'd be ready for a life of war once he made it to
Iraq. He was always adventurous and tough as a rattlesnake.
Guns came second nature to him. They felt natural in his
hands. Some like to say his sense of righteousness and adventure also came naturally, passed down through the generations.
Joe can trace his roots back to the legendary Pocahontas. If you
look him in the eyes then veer to his high cheekbones, you can
see the Pocahontas in him. "Pocahontas" was a nickname that
means "the naughty one" or "spoiled child" in the language of
the Powhatan. Pocahontas's real name was Matoaka. Jan likes
to kid about her husband's propensity to get into trouble, so she
might agree that Pocahontas and Joe share more than blood.

Once he settled in at Fort Drum, Joe shared a set of bunk
beds with a fellow named Joaquin Flores, a native of El Salvador. They became friends right away.

"What's your story?" Joe asked.

Joaquin told him that he worked as a long-haul truck driver whose routes stretched across the country.

"What got you here?"

"I joined because a kid from my hometown was killed." Joaquin said that the soldier inspired him to give something back to the country.

"Where do you live?"

When Joaquin told him "Armuchee," Joe stopped for a moment. He realized that Justin was the young soldier who changed Joaquin's life.

Thirty days after he reported to Fort Drum, the army placed Joe on a plane for the war zone. The flight to Kuwait was about fourteen hours with fueling stops in Iceland and Romania. He had a three-day layover in Kuwait before boarding a cargo plane to Iraq.

"It was a wild ride on a C-17 cargo plane," Joe said. "They fly kind of crazy to make themselves a harder target to hit."

Terrorists use rocket-propelled grenades and other arms to shoot at American aircraft. It's a real coup for the third-rate killers to hit one. They get their video cameras ready and dance around downed aircraft like its New Year's Day in New York.

Joe stayed at Camp Anaconda (forty-two miles north of Baghdad) for a day until a Chinook helicopter could give him a lift to Camp Al Taji (sixteen miles northwest of Baghdad). He finally arrived there about midnight.

"They didn't have a place for us to sleep, so I laid down on the gravel, I was so tired," he said.

A high-ranking officer apparently saw Joe on the ground, which didn't make for a good situation. The guy in charge of bunks lost his job.

Joe was assigned to trailers that could sleep six. Things didn't seem so tough. He was close to the laundry and the phones.

"Then I was issued my basic load of ammo that first day—240 rounds," Joe said. "Reality set in then; I knew it was starting to get serious."

The second day in country, Joe went on his first mission off base.

"When we left the wire, I wasn't scared," he said. "But I'd be lying if I said I wasn't nervous. IEDs were a big concern of mine, as it is of everybody that goes out the wire."

Joe was part of a security team that accompanied the civil affairs teams that attended Iraqi council meetings and generally checked on local officials to see if they needed assistance. Council meetings could get a little rough.

"They usually turned into a gripe session, some of them getting mad and walking out," Joe said.

Interpreters helped Joe and the others understand the Iraqis' needs and relayed intelligence on the terrorists. Sometimes Iraqis asked for the soldiers to build something new for them or to make improvements.

"The very first meeting I attended, we had a couple of other stops to make. We stopped at a school the U.S. was funding and at a bread store where some U.S. soldiers had mistakenly kicked in the door. We gave him a voucher to have it replaced," Joe said.

"On the way back to base we dropped off our interpreter at an Iraqi police station, and I found out that one of the Iraqi council members had been assassinated not long after he left the meeting."

Joe did security for elections while he was in Taji. "I think they were voting on a constitution," he said.

He did foot patrols in Husainiyah, which is next to Sadr City. Raw sewage ran in the streets. He couldn't walk without stepping in it. The sound of discharged weapons ricocheted through the city streets, but Joe didn't hear anything too close. Patrolling the streets in a Humvee, he had a different view. He sat in the gunner's turret, which is the uppermost point on the truck. He watched the children who spent their days in homes literally made of trash. On the ground, they would beg for food or water or a soldier's sunglasses or watches. Joe had a soft heart for the kids, and he gave his things away more than once. He couldn't stand to see the children suffering.

Joe was on security the entire time he was in Taji. The world in Iraq was so far away from Georgia—or any place in the United States. Other troops built roads and sewer systems that never existed before the Americans and coalition troops arrived.

"We aren't rebuilding anything—they're getting it for the first time," he said. "Most of the areas never had running water or sewage systems. You wouldn't believe how these people were living," Joe said. "None of the kids attended school, most were barefoot and some were totally naked. It was pitiful."

Despite his love for the kids, Joe never forgot why he was in Iraq. He left his wife and family to kill terrorists like the fiends who had murdered his son. Nothing against the kids. A silver-tone bracelet on his right wrist was an ever-present reminder of what he had lost and why he was in Iraq. The bracelet is inscribed with Justin's name and the date terrorists killed him. Joe intended to wear it every day he was in Iraq.

☆ ☆

JAN'S DAYS dragged on, tinged with fear. She was back to watching a lot of cable news. She worried all day about Joe, and then,

at night, she took sleeping pills so she could get a bit of rest. Joe tried to call her every day or e-mail, but sometimes things didn't work out.

Joe lied to Jan and told her that his job was guarding the gate at the base. He didn't want her to worry about him. He had put her through enough, and she loved him so much that she didn't kick up a fuss when he wanted to go to Iraq.

"Joe hates being inside the wire. He says the days are long," Jan said. "I told him the days are long for me when he's outside the wire."

Joe and Jan had moved from Rome to Lyerly, Georgia (about twenty-five miles northwest of Rome), on a chunk of land where their grandkids could play, they could grow huge gardens with tomatoes and beans, and Joe and the family could fish. They'd have to look out for the poisonous water moccasins, but that didn't scare them away. Joleen's family moved onto the land with Joe and Jan, so the grandkids were close.

Jan kept busy babysitting, comforting other families who had lost somebody in the war, and fulfilling a request from Joe.

"I want the deck finished when I come home," he said. "And one other request: I'd like to see a hot tub on the deck."

Jan could swing a hammer, nail down roof shakes, and pour a foundation. Plumbing was no problem, though it isn't her favorite trade. She could get a deck finished easily. But even with the projects and the grandbabies, she had time to worry.

One day she went into Rome and visited Justin's grave. Jan liked it to look nice. Others had come by and left knickknacks. It made Jan feel good that somebody else was visiting Justin. While she was there, she encountered the guy who oversees the cemetery.

"He asked how I was doing. I told him about Joe—then I asked if there were any more graves available," Jan said. "I

know if something happened to Joe that he would want to be buried by Justin."

The man told her that he would keep a grave site available, but he was sure she wouldn't need it.

EVERY DAY Joe heard gunfire and explosions. He had transferred to Al Asad (112 miles west of Baghdad), the largest base in Iraq. It has American amenities, like Subway sandwiches and Pizza Hut. Inside the wire, things weren't too dangerous. Every once in a while terrorists would fire toward the base, but they weren't very good shots. One day Joe was on his bunk, resting under a mini-tent he made with blankets, when he heard the unmistakable sound of incoming rockets. He stayed in his bunk. Later he found out that the terrorists had hit a plane. Nobody was hurt.

"They're getting to be better shots," he said.

When he was on duty outside of the wire, Joe's job was to stay in front of the convoys and look for explosives or any type of danger. He was a forward observer, the gunner. His eyes were the eyes of his convoy. If he missed a roadside bomb, somebody could die. Convoys of trucks can be miles long, and a trip to Jordan is three hundred miles each way. Soldiers protect civilian truck drivers who transport supplies for the military, including anything from water and gas to ammunition.

Crossing the vast desert between Al Asad and Jordan is like traversing the Wild West around the time of the Civil War. The highway is littered with trash and abandoned supply trucks whose guts have been burned. They look like the skeletons of lumbering dinosaurs that fell in their tracks. It's a highway of death. Insurgents and terrorists travel the highway hoping to

pirate a supply truck, kill Americans—or anybody helping an American. Between September 1 and November 11, 2005, thirty-seven roadside bombs hit convoys or were detected by soldiers before they detonated. America's fiercest and most determined enemies roam the route, including al Qaeda in Iraq and Ansar al-Sunna.

Joe searched the highway for anything that could explode. Terrorists stuffed dead animals with bombs. These needed to be shot to detonate anything before an unsuspecting person was killed. Sometimes all you see is a shot-up pile of rotten flesh. But missing an IED can be a fatal mistake, as Joe knows all too well.

What he really wanted was a chance to kill a terrorist, a bomb builder who aimed to kill somebody else's son.

ON SLOW nights inside his tent, Joe taught himself Arabic. He made flash cards so he could learn how to tell Iraqis that he was there to help them.

"I wanted them to know that America was good. We are here to help them," he said.

The Iraqis were usually friendly to Joe and the other soldiers. Every once in a while he'd run into somebody who didn't like Americans. One night while on foot patrol, a boy approached Joe on the street. Joe figured he'd want candy or sunglasses.

"He said, 'F— you, soldier. F— Americans.' I told him that it wasn't nice to cuss like that and didn't his parents teach him nothing. He said, 'F— you.'"

Kids sometimes packed weapons, so an angry little cuss wasn't anything to ignore. He sent the kid on his way and watched for aggressive movements.

Joe got a kick out of the benign kids with potty mouths. They were rebellious, but he didn't like the fact that they might grow up to be suicide bombers or another style of terrorist.

The first days Joe was in Iraq, he called Jan when he could. She would catch him up on news of home. And Jan was keeping an eye on Cindy Sheehan, who was stirring up a lot of bad feelings among the families whose loved ones were overseas or had died in the war.

CAMP CASEY

Someone said . . . "We should go down in a pasture near
Bush's ranch and thousands of people would come and you
ought to call it 'Turdstock'—so let's call it Turdstock."
—*Cindy Sheehan*[1]

CINDY AND HER FAMILY had always opposed the war in Iraq.
Before Casey left for the war front, Cindy offered to take
him to Canada as a conscientious objector. He declined. Casey
had made a commitment to his country and his army buddies,
and he would follow through on it. Besides, he loved being a
soldier.

Family and friends visited with Casey in December 2003
before his deployment. The quiet man was a fit soldier who had
just signed another contract with the army. Again, Casey failed
to speak to his parents about extending his duty to the U.S.
Army. As close as he was with his family, he chose not to dis-
cuss his career moves with them.

"He looked happy and very healthy," said Liz Kroman,
Cindy's best friend.

Four months later, the sight of Casey lying in a casket crushed Cindy, ultimately shaking her into activism. She spent sleepless nights on the Internet searching for answers and for others who might know something of her grief. She considered killing herself when the pain stole her ability to breathe steady or eat or sleep.

"For many nights after Casey was killed and we buried him, I had to restrain myself from swallowing my entire bottle of sleeping pills. The pain and the deep pit of hopelessness and despair were almost more than I could cope with," she said.[2]

Cindy's grief took her further and further away from her family. She didn't eat much or go outside. She holed up in a room where she suffered from dark and disturbing issues that arise in people who won't face their grief head on or who may suffer from other psychological problems. They dodge it and, in ways they can't explain, run from it. Though it may seem selfish, it feels better to relate to strangers who don't know about your pain than to a husband or child who know too well the crushing darkness of death.

But she chose to live because of her three surviving children. Cindy would not inflict more grief on them. But she decided to fight back against the Bush administration and what she calls the "war machine."

The road from Cow Town to Crawford was long.

Months before she sat in a ditch outside President Bush's Texas ranch, Cindy had protested in the streets of Benicia, California, one of Solano County's seven cities and close to Vacaville. Pat Kniesler met Cindy in Benicia during the earlier days of Cindy's transition toward full-time protesting. Kniesler had been motivated to act by what she considered an unjust war, and so she joined the Solano Peace and Justice folks to protest.

"It was my first vigil—I was scared to death," Kniesler said.

She kept going back and carrying signs with the number of Americans listed who had died in Iraq. After watching the numbers climb, she decided that she should start a Web site to track the deaths so the world could see.

In December 2004, Kniesler e-mailed Cindy and the two hooked up. Cindy went to Benicia and marched with the group. Cindy was already seasoned as a protester and public speaker. She became involved in protest on Independence Day in 2004, when she and her sister, Dede Miller, went to a gathering in Berkeley. Miller described the meeting to Melanie Morgan in an e-mail:

> We went to a function at the Unitarian Church in Berkeley on 07/04/04. Cindy had been corresponding with two other parents who had lost kids in Iraq. They were speaking at the church. That is when our activism began.
>
> We founded Gold Star Families for Peace in Dec 04, 8 months after Casey died. It was formed out of the realization that the war would one day or another end but Gold Star Families would always be Gold Star Families.

Cindy didn't oppose all war.

"I have always been against killing, but I was of the view that maybe some wars were justified, and I am now 'no war'— that killing to solve problems is not justifiable, it's not the way to solve problems, it's not the solution. To me, that my views are extremist in my country is very ironic," Cindy told an Irish journalist.[3]

After she got her feet wet, Cindy lambasted President Bush, Secretary of Defense Donald Rumsfeld, media outlets,

journalists, some Vacaville residents, and anybody else who offended her mission.

Regulars at Stars Bowling Alley in Vacaville knew early on that Cindy and her daughter, Carly, had worked for John Kerry's 2004 presidential campaign. Cindy and Carly had both worked at the bowling alley, which is a gathering spot for all ages. Both spoke openly about their grief over Casey's death and how they blamed President Bush for the tragedy. Their close friends at work tried to comfort the Sheehans and witnessed their grief turn into bitterness. They listened as Carly talked about her mother's ties to Kerry. Everything changed after the release of Michael Moore's *Fahrenheit 911*, which took on the president and America's war on terror.

"One week after *Fahrenheit 911* debuted, Carly began traveling with the John Kerry campaign," said a close friend and confidante of the Sheehan women. "Before she left to travel, she began recruiting friends at Stars and other acquaintances to the campaign. She passed out business cards with her name on them and her title, media coordinator for Realvoices.com."

Carly bragged to folks at the bowling alley that Kerry's campaign had hired her mom and her and that they traveled with the candidate at his expense. The grieving pair would work to wreck President Bush's standing on the war in Iraq. Other grief-stricken parents, including the Johnsons, were also contacted by anti-Bush operatives who tried recruiting them for the Kerry campaign.

"Carly was involved and had been offered a job, but I don't think it ever really evolved into much money. They enticed her with a job, then mostly wanted her to volunteer, but I know she definitely campaigned for Kerry with her mother," said Cherie Quartarolo, Pat Sheehan's sister and Casey's aunt and godmother.

Cindy and Carly made anti-Bush commercials as part of the Real Voices campaign in which they questioned why Casey had to die in the Iraq War. Cindy was determined to do all she could to defeat the president's reelection effort and went to Florida toward the end of the 2004 presidential campaign. Her campaigning hurt her in-laws.

"My parents feel that they were not allowed to grieve properly. They would see their daughter-in-law [Cindy] on the evening news with photos of their grandson as a baby, a fake coffin, chanting political statements and campaigning for a presidential candidate," Cherie said. "It was too surreal for them, very painful. They could not grieve in private in their own home with this invasion. It was at about this time Cindy announced she would never speak to any of the Sheehan family if they voted for Bush, also saying, 'If you vote for Bush, you killed Casey.'"

In Vacaville, Cindy's friends noted other changes in her personality after she hit the national stage with the Real Voices campaign.

"Cindy, you've changed since the Kerry campaign contacted you in early July of last summer. You're not the same grieving mom, especially after you started traveling on the road to support John Kerry's campaign," a friend wrote on a blog in late September 2005. The friend noted that her daughter and Cindy were very close and that her daughter had spent hours helping Cindy after Casey's death.

"You've turned into a political puppet for those who are exploiting you and it's not pretty nor does it do anything for Casey's memory," the friend added.

Despite her clear connections to Kerry, Cindy insisted that the Democrats were not using her. She did not want anybody to

think she was a political pawn. A Web site set up to honor Casey included the statement: "Real Voices is a nonprofit organization that spends 100 percent of its donations on effective political action. They advocate the election of John Kerry but are not affiliated with his campaign."[4] This statement was very important to comply with campaign finance laws. But politicians learn quickly how to skirt such laws, and one of the ways is to use a nonprofit to attack an opponent so that the campaign has no fingerprints on the political hit.

In the case of Real Voices and Cindy Sheehan, the connections to the Kerry campaign are undeniable. The clearest link is Scott Rafferty, who worked on Kerry's steering committee and as his attorney for the California campaign.[5] Rafferty was knee-deep in Real Voices.

After its inception in July 2004, Real Voices immediately began having problems with the Federal Elections Commission. Real Voices' officers repeatedly failed to file required forms, such as the statement of organization and the group's expenses. The FEC threatened the group with an audit or other "enforcement action," according to FEC documents.

The statement of organization, which helps the federal government track affiliations, was eventually filed. It showed that Real Voices indeed had links to an unnamed federal candidate and that it was not a separate "segregated fund or party committee."

After more FEC threats, Rafferty contacted the agency and settled the grievances. It was clear then that Kerry was directly linked to Real Voices and Cindy through his campaign's California attorney and Cindy's blatant campaigning for Kerry.

After George Bush was reelected, Cindy regretted that she had worked for Kerry's campaign. "I will not support a pro-war

LEFT: Casey Sheehan, sixteen months old, was very happy and giggly at this age, according to his family.

This 1994 photograph shows the Sheehan family. Fourteen-year-old Casey stands between his father, Pat, and his mother, Cindy.

RIGHT: Casey Sheehan stands next to the First Cavalry insignia at Fort Irwin. He had desert training in early 2004, a few months before terrorists killed him on April 4, 2004.

ABOVE LEFT: Justin Johnson was born with little hair, but once it came in, it was a head full of curls. ABOVE RIGHT: Joe and Justin spend some time together.

BELOW: The Johnson family is baptized together in the Armuchee Creek.

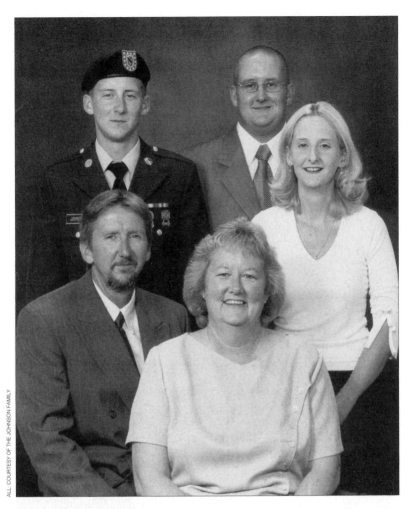

Justin Johnson wears his army uniform in this picture of the family. Brother Joshua stands next to Justin. Jan is seated with Joe (left) and Joleen (right).

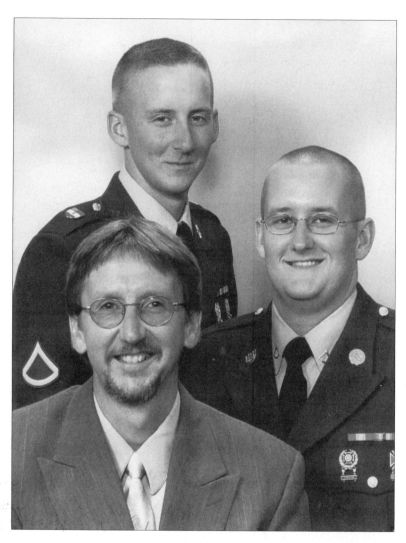

Joe regrets not getting a picture of all three of the Johnson men in their Class A's before Justin died. Justin is standing; Joshua is next to Joe.

Justin and Joe Johnson held the same job in the army. Justin is pictured below in his turret. Later, a friend took a picture of Joe (above) in his turret atop a Humvee.

ABOVE: Joe Johnson shares some time with Iraqi children. He enjoyed giving them watches and sunglasses. The children helped soften his broken heart.

Jan shows Joe Johnson for the first time the memorial magnet on his brand-new truck. Joe was home for R&R.

Joe poses in front of a massive pockmarked portrait of Saddam Hussein (right) in Baghdad. Riflemen have erased the dictator's face.

BOTTOM OF FACING PAGE: Joe's granddaughter Jordan holds a picture she drew of her Da, her nickname for Joe. Her heart broke when Justin died, and she was angry at Da for going to war.

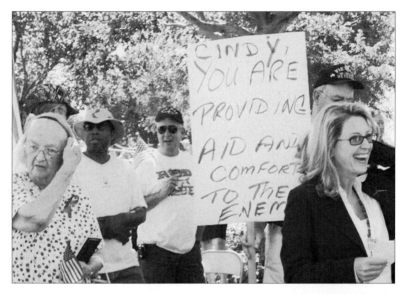

Vacaville residents protest against supporters of Cindy Sheehan, then a fellow Vacaville resident, during the summer of 2005.

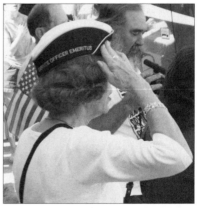

Democrat. I regret supporting John Kerry in 2004," she said. "The movement gained *nothing* from his candidacy."[6]

She hooked up with Moveon.org, the leftist organization funded by billionaire George Soros, and did a commercial in the campaign against a second term for President Bush. She gave speeches on March 19, 2005, at a peace rally outside of Fort Bragg; on April 4, 2005, at Riverside Church in New York; and on June 16, 2005, at a forum held by liberal Rep. John Conyers (D-MI) in Washington, D.C., on the controversial Downing Street memo that raised questions among some critics about how President Bush chose to go to war.

Cindy felt like the peace movement wasn't gaining the traction she wanted. She had spent almost a year trying to oust what she called the "murderous thugs" running the U.S. government. Then, on August 5, 2005, the tide turned for Cindy and her rage against the machine. She said she had a "brainstorm"[7] to go to Crawford while she was writing an e-mail to friends. Cindy would demand to meet again with President Bush to publicly browbeat him by asking for what noble cause Casey had died. It struck a cord with news types in a summer doldrums. What could be more heartfelt than the story of a grieving mother's plea to meet with the policymakers who had sent her son to die in a war she deemed unjust? Little notice, however, was made that, unlike most parents whose sons or daughters had been killed in the war, Cindy had already met with the president.

Cindy and Pat met with President Bush at Fort Lewis, Washington, along with sixteen other families in June 2004. The military gave the Sheehans the VIP treatment, flying them at no cost and ensuring their comfort at the base.

After ten minutes alone with the president, both Cindy and Pat said that he had been respectful and kind to them. Cindy

told the *Vacaville Reporter* that—despite disagreeing with Bush on the war—she was happy with the meeting.

"I know now he's sincere about wanting freedom for the Iraqis," Cindy said. "I know he's sorry and feels some pain for our loss. And I know he's a man of faith."[8]

Most parents whose children die in Iraq don't get a chance to meet the president. Joe and Jan Johnson never met with him. Jan even visited the tiny town of Crawford in 2006 after attending a memorial service for the soldiers at Fort Hood and hoped to see the president—or at least see the road leading to his home.

"It always made me angry that Cindy wanted a second meeting with the president and most of us Gold Star parents never had a first meeting," Jan said. "Don't our sons matter? Does she think she deserves two meetings instead of one of us getting one?"

In 2005, Cindy already had plans to be in Dallas for a speech at the Veterans for Peace convention. As soon as she sent the e-mail, people responded in droves. The media weren't far behind, thanks to Team Cindy, which brought sophisticated communications equipment to Crawford, including satellites, to get her message out.

On August 6, 2005, Cindy and twelve media-savvy anti-Bush buddies drove to Crawford in their "Impeachment Tour Bus." Dozens more stood by to support the protest. This was no spur-of-the-moment decision. Cindy and her colleagues were better equipped than seasoned Boy Scouts. They brought tents that they pitched in a ditch some three miles or so from the president's Crawford ranch, and they dubbed the encampment Camp Casey. Bush was resting and working at the ranch.

Though she no longer considered herself a Christian, Cindy and her supporters erected hundreds of white crosses in

a ditch next to the road leading to President Bush's ranch and near the spot where Cindy had initially camped. Each cross bore a plain paper tag, and each tag displayed the name of a soldier killed in Iraq. Many parents of the deceased soldiers objected to Cindy using their children's names in her campaign against the president and the war.

As her protest mushroomed under the glare of widespread media coverage and was nurtured by larger antiwar groups, Cindy's crews set up a graveyard of crosses near Camp Casey with the names of American men and women who died in Iraq. The media used shots of the crosses to publicize the argument that U.S. troops were suffering major casualties in the war that seemed to have no end in sight.

Her hometown newspaper, the *Vacaville Reporter*, fell into the vortex of the brewing storm because a reporter had written about the Sheehans' visit with the president in June 2004. Matt Drudge, the Web's master of ceremonies and news (www.drudgereport .com), published a report that Cindy had changed her mind on matters of the war. Inquiring minds went to the *Reporter* to look into its archives for past stories on Cindy. The newspaper had generally supported Cindy, except for columns by conservative columnist Catherine Moy, who was the first to criticize Cindy in an editorial piece. Editor Diane Barney wrote a column stating that Cindy had not changed her mind, a position Cindy later used to bolster her own credibility. But Moy followed up with a column pointing out that, while Cindy was consistent in her antiwar position, her views of the president had changed dramatically.

Casey's grandparents, paternal aunts and uncles, and other relatives were dismayed when she chose to make her stand in Texas. Their hearts still ached in mourning for Casey. Cindy

disagreed with her husband's family on many political issues, including their support of President Bush. She felt strongly that they had betrayed her when they voted for the president after Casey's death. Death in a family magnifies disagreements, stinging like the proverbial salt in open wounds. Finally, Cindy's in-laws could no longer stay silent as she protested Bush near his personal residence. They wrote an e-mail to Melanie Morgan that was later distributed to Matt Drudge (the text of the e-mail appears on page 172).

The e-mail exposed the Sheehan family to the scorn of leftists. Antiwar activists hoped that Cindy's status as a grieving parent would protect her from criticism. It is painful to criticize a woman who has lost her son, who has suffered a numbing loss. The same protective shield apparently does not cover other family members in mourning. Bloggers attacked the Sheehan family with their claws extended.

Liberal blogs at first questioned whether Casey's relatives really opposed Cindy. After Cindy confirmed that Cherie Quartarolo was her sister-in-law, they began more personal attacks.

"This 'announcement' was sent via e-mail to Drudge. Any one of us could have sent this message. Drudge does not indicate that he, in anyway confirmed the validity of the missive but since the Aunt in question (if she exists) sent it to Drudge that would certainly say a lot about her particular leanings as well as the intended audience, i.e. Wingnuts," Neoeconomist wrote.[9]

Liberal bloggers did not want to accept that Casey had relatives who supported either the war or President Bush.

"How can someone choose to support a retard like Bush over their own family? Boggles the mind. What has this country become?" Frank Emesis wrote on attytood.com.[10]

☆ ☆

AUGUST 8, 2005, Cindy's third day in Crawford, was overcast with dark skies and threatening weather. Texas thunderstorms famously throw lightning and thunder from the heavens as if Zeus himself hurled the angry energy. Cindy and her crew went into town and took cover at the Crawford Peace House, a meeting place and ground zero for local antiwar, anti-Bush activity.

Texans don't kid around when they talk about big. Storms, fire ants, snakes, land, trucks, and controversy are some of the big things one can easily find in the Lone Star State. Cindy's run-ins with Mother Nature grew each day until, on her fifth day, she abandoned the camp again to avoid the sweeping rains and to heal herself. She suffered a sore throat and fever.

In the meantime, her publicity machine was in full swing, bringing in one-sided interviews with major media and money. Lots of money. By Day Five in Crawford, the Peace House had received thirty thousand dollars.[11]

Pushing all of the right buttons for Cindy was a cadre of liberal, Marxist, and Communist organizations adept at manipulating the media, which was hungry for news in the dry news months of August. Among those helping Cindy's Crawford protest morph into an orgy of Bush whacking were:

- CodePink, a woman's antiwar group whose members wear Pepto Bismol–colored shirts, supported Cindy. Founder Medea Benjamin also started the San Francisco–based human rights organization Global Exchange, which begat the United for Peace and Justice (UPJ) coalition, the steam behind antiwar protests around the country before they hooked up with Cindy. Leslie Cagan, who touts extensive

activism with the American Communist Party, helped lead UPJ. During the last week of December 2004—eight months after Casey's death—Medea announced that her groups would send six hundred thousand dollars to Iraqi insurgents in Fallujah. She blames the United States for the hatred other countries have for Americans. CodePink distributed pink umbrellas to protesters needing protection from the blistering Texas sun.

- Lisa Fithian, a well-known political organizer who has played major roles in the violent protests against the World Trade Organization in Seattle and other antiglobalism around the world, believes each protest deserves different styles of action, which might include violence. Fithian was with Cindy from Day One, helping her organize the media event. "Fithian is a sign of how far Cindy Sheehan has strayed from the roots of her 'one mom' crusade against George W. Bush. Or, perhaps more accurately, it is a sign that the 'one mom' crusade was never just one mom," Byron York wrote in the *National Review.*[12]

- Fenton Communications is infamous for its work in the now-debunked Alar apple scare in the late 1980s and other junk science later found to be unreliable. Journalist Jennifer Verner observed, "The radical Left owes a great debt of gratitude to David Fenton. He has mixed Neo-Marxist ideology with junk science, trial lawyers, labor, progressive millionaires, politicians, and radical policy wonks to construct a complex, moneymaking left-wing advocacy empire. Fenton Communications reported billing $6 million in 2002 and will likely make much more this year with

high profile clients like The Heinz Family Foundation
(John Kerry's wife, Theresa Heinz's foundation), the afore-
mentioned Open Society Institute and Moveon.org. . . .
Fenton was also a member of the White Panther Party (a
Caucasian-led offshoot of the Black Panthers), and even
did photography work for the Weathermen, the Commu-
nist/anarchist group which bombed the U.S. Capitol build-
ing, along with other prominent U.S. institutions in
Washington, DC and New York City."[13] As the mouthpiece
for the Real Voices campaign, which included Cindy and
other families who have lost loved ones in the Iraq War,
Fenton Communications also worked to get John Kerry
elected.

- True Majority, a liberal activist organization founded by
 Ben Cohen of Ben and Jerry's Ice Cream, paid for Fenton
 Communications' help in Crawford.

Cindy was never alone in Crawford, and her friends were
happy to feed the mainstream media.

MEDIA GONE WILD

News Hounds is upset at me for seeming to hang up on Bill Kristol, the chickenhawk-in-chief. But really, folks, a fear of confronting neocons and other warmongers is not among my failings.

—*Cindy Sheehan*[1]

AUGUST IS NOT A good month for the news media. Congress is out of session, so lawmakers aren't making headlines. Traditional public schools aren't teaching children, so education reporters can't look for stories there. Television and newspaper editors are begging for a good story.

By June 2005, Americans were becoming war weary. For the first time since the Iraq War began in March 2003, 52 percent of Americans polled in a *Washington Post*–ABC poll released on June 8, 2005, said that they believed the war did not make them safer. About 60 percent said that the war was no longer worth fighting and blamed the Bush administration for the perceived failures that a drop in the president's poll numbers (52 percent disapproved of how Bush was handling his job). The mood of the country worked as a perfect backdrop for Cindy to attack

Two months later, Cindy camped down the road from the

president's ranch. The media and many Americans saw her as a heartbroken mother who deeply grieved her son's death and merely wanted simple answers to her questions. She wanted to know why the president had sent her son to war. Cindy was acting out what the polls were showing: Americans were turning against the war, the media needed a good story, and Cindy loved the media. She offered great sound bytes for the evening news and offered a mourning face that nobody wanted to debate.

Fenton Communications and Lisa Fithian knew they had a winner with Cindy. They scheduled national and international interviews for her, took phone calls, and answered her e-mails. By Day Three in Crawford's hellish heat, Cindy's professional media handlers scored.

"I conservatively got 3 to 5 phone calls a minute," Cindy wrote in her daily blog. "I did about 25 phone interviews and several TV interviews. I did several right-wing radio interviews. I was supposed to do: The Today Show, MSNBC live interview, Connected Coast to Coast (MSNBC) and Hardball (MSNBC). The Today Show just never showed up and the other 3 MSNBC shows cancelled for no reason. Could it be because NBC is owned by General Electric, a major defense contractor??"[2]

Still, the professional media relations worked, and Cindy got her message out. She was the perfect figurehead for the antiwar crowd. She had suffered a cruel loss, and now she wanted an answer. The media were cooperative and offered little cross-examination or criticism—at least in the early days of Crawford. At first, even conservative talk-show host Rush Limbaugh wouldn't criticize or question her motives on-air. Later, the godfather of talk radio ramped up the criticism as Cindy's campaign stretched into weeks.

Bloggers weighed in with heavy criticism, as did other talk-

show hosts. Some attacked with the brutality usually reserved for public officials and enemies of state. One nationally syndicated talk-show host dubbed Cindy the "bitch in the ditch," which was mild compared to the language appearing on the Web.

Cindy's critics also received a heavy load of crass, hateful e-mails. Crazies even threatened to kill some of her high-profile detractors.

Death threats rolled in to the family of Mark Williams, a libertarian radio personality in Sacramento, California, who had serious problems with Cindy's position on the war. E-mailers and bloggers promised to kill Williams's dog Casey, the mascot for a charity called Casey's Kids to Kids, which the Williams family had started for Iraqi schoolchildren and orphans.

"These people are no better than terrorists! It takes a sick person to threaten a little dog for being a symbol of hope for hungry children," said Holly Williams, Mark's wife.

Nobody who spoke strongly on either side of the debate was immune to attacks as bitter as raw cucumbers and as vile as Satan himself. Cindy's demands and self-described occupation of Crawford poured gas on the debate over the war on terror in Iraq. The media lapped it up, and bloggers kept a wary eye on media bias. The whole world chimed in. Cindy's blogs about her protest in Crawford appeared on several Web sites, including Michael Moore's, Arianna Huffington's, and DailyKos.com.

Steve Janke writes blogs from Canada at his aptly named site, "Angry in the Great White North." He followed Cindy's story like a hound on a raccoon. His grasp of the situation and connections to Cindy's extended family placed him in the center of the Cindy tsunami.

"I read about Cindy and found a lot of logical and legal fallacies," Janke said. He researched some of the folks helping Cindy

in Crawford and questioned why none of the affiliations had been mentioned in any mainstream articles. Were they afraid of criticizing a woman who'd lost her son, or was it that they agreed with her and wanted to legitimize her position?

"It was probably the media's fault," Janke said.

New York Times columnist Maureen Dowd on August 10, 2005, wrote that Cindy had complete moral authority to question the war because Casey had died in the war. Dowd threw down the gauntlet, warning others in the media that Cindy was above reproach.

But the questions kept coming from influential writers such as Christopher Hitchens, the acid-tongued former leftist whose political persuasion has slowly morphed into something only Chris Hitchens could explain. Hitchens is a relentless fact-checker when it comes to the moral depravity of the Saddam Hussein regime and cannot be fooled by ideologues on the Right and the Left.

His writings leave no doubt that he stands against dictators and despots, punks and thug killers, and that his native England and adopted country of America have the right and the responsibility to stop genocide when it is encountered.

Five days after Dowd's column, Hitchens went on offense:

Sheehan has obviously taken a short course in the Michael Moore/Ramsey Clark school of Iraq analysis and has not succeeded in making it one atom more elegant or persuasive. I dare say that her "moral authority" to do this is indeed absolute, if we agree for a moment on the weird idea that moral authority is required to adopt overtly political positions, but then so is my "moral" right to say that she is spouting sinister piffle. Suppose I had lost a child in this war. Would any of my

critics say that this gave me any extra authority? I certainly would not ask or expect them to do so. Why, then, should anyone grant them such a privilege?[3]

Cindy's handlers were careful not to book her with "hostile" media after a couple of "bad" interviews. Even the friendly outlets that tested Cindy's authority as Mother Sheehan were ignored or booted. That's what happened to National Public Radio on August 29, 2005, when reporter Neil Conan asked questions that Cindy didn't like.

At first, things were as cordial as high-noon tea at Buckingham Palace. Then it started to feel like a White House press conference in the middle of Watergate, according to transcripts of the exchange:

NEIL CONAN (NC): Um, and of course, I don't want to get too personal, but . . . I wonder: When he was deciding to join the army, did you try to talk him out of it?

CINDY SHEEHAN (CS): We didn't have a chance because he joined before he talked to us.

NC: Before he talked. So, he made a choice of his own.

CS: (Pause) Right.

NC: Um, now, you were . . .

CS: (Not so cheerfully) But what does that have to do with him being sent to a war that's illegal and immoral to kill people and get killed for, um, a country that was no threat or harm to the United States of America?

NC: Uh . . . no. But, he wasn't drafted. He made a choice of free will.

CS: Yeah, and if we give our children to the government to serve their country, we should make sure that they're only

used if it's absolutely necessary to defend the United
States of America.

NC: I wonder, now, you got a chance to meet with President
Bush with a group of other families for a brief time. What
happened in that meeting?

CS: Um . . . I've talked about this a lot. Do we have to talk
about this? Do you have any questions about what's going
on right now or what we're gonna do in the future?

NC: I'm just curious; I've not heard your answer to this.

CS: Um, excuse me?

NC: I've not heard your answer, if you wouldn't mind.

CS: (someone speaking in background) I have two minutes.

NC: (amazed) You have two minutes?

CS: I have two minutes so . . . he was—George Bush acted
like we were at a tea party, he was rude to us, and we felt
worse than we did after we met him.

NC: Mm hm. Um, I didn't realize you just had two minutes.
We thought we had more time with you today, but, uh . . .
I did want to ask. I know you're planning to, when Presi-
dent Bush comes back to Washington, you're planning to
continue the protest here in Washington.

Cindy continued for another minute or so and answered a
question about other Gold Star parents who disagree with her.
When Conan asked a final question about some of Cindy's state-
ments, she said she had to go and ended the call. Conan was
dumbfounded by her swift exit.

NC: Cindy Sheehan. Leaving us there in Crawford, Texas.
We apologize for that. We had arranged with people
there to speak with Cindy Sheehan for the remainder of

this segment and take some phone calls as well. Uh, evidently, plans changed at the last minute and we apologize for that.[4]

Cindy made a practice of staying off the Fox cable network. She called it the "Ministry of Propaganda for the Republicans."[5] She did agree to a Fox morning show, which she believed was a local affiliate, she said. But then she recognized the voice of Bill Kristol, a conservative who disagreed adamantly with Cindy.

"When I realized, upon hearing the dreaded Kristol Jr. moniker, that I was on national Fox, I was outta there. I had many people, including actual journalists, waiting to talk to me, after all," Cindy wrote in her explanation for hanging up on Kristol.[6]

The Fox morning personalities were perplexed, because they had already asked questions of Cindy and she had answered. The audience also tossed a couple her way. And she answered. Then Kristol came on and, voilà, Cindy was gone. She claimed she had more legitimate media with whom to speak.

Back in Vacaville, where Cindy's family still lived, the hometown newspaper's editorial pages started to show some cracks in the "we love Cindy" peace parade. Letters criticizing some of Cindy's rhetoric rolled in to the *Vacaville Reporter's* editor. Vacaville residents had supported the Sheehans in every way possible, from helping to pay funeral costs to remodeling their home at no charge. But some were hurt that Cindy had seemingly moved on and forgotten the good they had done. Even before Cindy took her stand in Crawford, her former friends and neighbors began to speak up.

Gordy Calder was one of the fellows who helped spruce up

the Sheehan home after Casey's death. In a letter to the editor on June 27, 2005, he addressed the issue:

> Thank you to all the craftsmen who worked with me on the Sheehan family home in memory of Army Spc. Casey Sheehan. I want to personally thank the electrician, painter, tile installer, floor and carpet installer, and plumber, and also those who provided the flooring, windows and cabinets. As far as I know, all volunteered labor and lots of material. Cindy Sheehan has been very busy and did not have time to thank you all.

Cindy began blaming the mainstream media for her publicity troubles. She had a love-hate relationship with her hometown newspaper, which gladly ran articles she submitted to explain her position. Her anger boiled over to the point that she stopped talking with the *Vacaville Reporter,* which published an editorial explaining the blowup.

> It has not been our news coverage that has infuriated Mrs. Sheehan during the past year; rather, it has been many letters to the editor critical of her campaign.
> Sure, there were positive letters as well, not to mention at least three essays authored by Mrs. Sheehan. But the criticisms hit hard. For a while, she wasn't returning our phone calls, although she granted interviews with national media. She later admitted that each time we wrote about her, it sparked a spate of painful letters for her and her family.
> She later resumed responding to calls and e-mails, but has repeatedly expressed her disappointment with letters, at one time thanking *The Reporter* "for making me feel like a pariah in my own community."[7]

CINDY'S INTERNATIONAL campaign saturated newspapers and cable television and network newscasts. Pictures of her kneeling by makeshift graves or crosses with tears streaming down her face popped up around the world.

Bloggers dissected photographs to show the media favored Cindy's take on the Iraq War. One example went around the Internet that showed Cindy and the Reverend Al Sharpton "grieving" together. It was a solemn, tight shot with their faces grimacing as they shared time together. The image appeared in many U.S. newspapers. Bloggers paired it with a wider shot that showed television microphones boomed over the grieving pair and a gaggle of reporters following the two like lost goslings.[8] The photograph told two different stories, and the media favored the story of a grieving mother being consoled by a civil rights activist.

DESPITE SOME rough spots early on, Cindy and the media got along pretty well. They needed each other during the late days of 2005. The media had their news features, and Cindy and the antiwar movement received wall-to-wall publicity and what they believed was new energy to fight President Bush and the supporters of the war in Iraq.

Eleven days into her Crawford stay, Cindy was transformed from a homemaker and former youth minister to the world's most famous grieving mother. According to the Video Monitoring Service, her name had been mentioned 20,585 times in television news broadcasts. Cindy was reaching cult status.

SCORES OF flower arrangements, love notes, money, and celebrities showed up in Texas for Cindy. Rep. John Conyers (D-MI) wrote a letter asking the president to meet again with Cindy. Five other liberal congresspeople signed the letter.

Actors went to Cindy's side to lambaste the president. Months after Cindy's visit to Crawford, Jane Fonda said that she had stepped aside as America's most noted antiwar activist to make way for Cindy. "I wanted to do a tour like I did during the Vietnam War, a tour of the country," the Oscar-winning actress said. "But then Cindy Sheehan filled in the gap, and she is better at this than I am. I carry too much baggage."[9]

Fonda lunched with Cindy and her daughters in the fall of 2005. The actress counseled the girls on how to handle their mother's celebrity and the jabs by her critics. This meeting did not make headlines. It was best for Cindy's campaign that Fonda stayed under the radar. Many Americans and veterans still believe that Fonda betrayed America when she posed on a North Vietnamese antiaircraft weapon during the Vietnam War. The pose earned her the pejorative nickname "Hanoi Jane."

Fonda did not stand by Cindy's side in Crawford, but she was there in spirit. Others in the antiwar crowd looked to Cindy as a spiritual leader. They wept with her, prayed with her, sang with her, and defended her. Cindy Sheehan was no longer just a grieving mother. She was Mother Sheehan, a near deity who had given her son as the martyr to their movement. One Internet regular, known as dataguy, suggested:

We should call her "Mother Sheehan." . . . "Mother Sheehan" is her title, and expresses her ceremonial status as a bereaved mother, calling forth over the dead body of her son. She is not a person now, she is a mother, which is not an expression of her in-

dividuality, but rather the expression of her eternal character: the mother, the bringer of life who has been wronged by state power.

Mother Sheehan became the subject of paintings and writings and invitations from the rich and famous. Nobel laureate Dario Fo, a leftist playwright, wrote "Peace Mom" to portray Cindy's fight against the war. The one-woman show premiered in London in December 2005 with a backdrop of Casey's pictures and a tank in the Iraqi desert.

For some, a meeting with Cindy was of the highest spiritual order, something akin to meeting the pope or Mother Teresa or Mohandas Gandhi. Howie Klein, the former president of Reprise Records and a gay activist, had such an experience with Cindy.

I prepared for my August trip to Crawford, Texas, not by digging out my f dubya T-shirt that a friend had brought back from Bolivia or Cuba or England. Instead, I went into abstinence mode. . . . I purged my consciousness as best I could of the profane and worldly preoccupations that dwell there. I fasted for 48 hours, eating nothing and drinking only water and even forgoing my dozens of herbal supplements.[10]

According to his first-person account, Klein never let his mind wander to George Bush, whom he blamed for Cindy's grief. He fasted and kept his mind steady so he could face the hometown of Bush. For him, this journey was akin to entering Mephistopheles' lair:

But I was fasting and meditating and getting ready to travel to the hometown of George Bush—surely the most detested individual in the world, probably the individual most hated by the

largest numbers of people anytime in history, more reviled than Hitler or Stalin or Genghis Khan were in their times![11]

BY THE end of August, three out of four Americans knew about Cindy Sheehan. She may have been the media's darling, but Joe and Jane America had different ideas. Americans who disagreed with Cindy's message were preparing a reply.

"YOU DON'T SPEAK FOR ME, CINDY!

I wanted to go to Crawford to show my support. A mother—
the local Cindy Sheehan—asked if I was going to Crawford. I
said that if I did, I'd be sitting on the opposite side of Cindy
Sheehan. But Joe was getting ready to go to Iraq, so I was in
New York to say good-bye.

—*Jan Johnson*

CINDY DUG IN FOR a long stay in Crawford. Aside from the
blistering, wet heat, Crawford was relatively comfortable
for the Vacaville mother. Personal assistants answered her e-
mails and scheduled her days, which included massages and
catered meals. She received flowers and small gifts from folks
around the country, and the mainstream media loved her.

But Cindy's demands and raw language irritated some
Americans. Pro-troops organizations around the country
planned a major rebuttal. Kristinn Taylor of FreeRepublic.com
helped a Texas chapter of the conservative group organize a rally
to show the world that the antiwar crowd was out of touch with
most of America.

Nine days before the rally, on August 27, 2005, Move Amer-
ica Forward (MAF)—a nonpartisan, nonprofit organization

with primarily conservative leaders—went into a frenzy of activity. Their mission: support the troops and defend America. They made plans to convoy into Crawford to demonstrate support for the soldiers in Iraq and their families and the president.

Move America Forward already had a history with Cindy Sheehan's antiwar message. Members of MAF had seen Cindy up-close for the first time on a rainy evening in April 2005 in Sacramento, when a crowd of agitated protesters on both sides of the Iraq War converged. They had stood vigil where well-known Bay Area peace activists Stephen and Virginia Pearcy hanged an American soldier in effigy from the rafters of their home. The act had infuriated the Pearcys' neighbors, Gold Star family members, and many who had read about it in their local papers and had heard about it on talk radio.

That night, Cindy Sheehan debuted her story on local television. She appeared to be more angry than grieving and sounded like a Valley girl with a high-pitched voice. Move America Forward took note of her. Its principals—including Sal Russo, Joe Wierzbicki, and Melanie Morgan—could see with frightening clarity that the Left was gaining traction in the debate on the war. The White House was not fighting back. The Bush administration was conceding the argument that there had been no weapons of mass destruction, though it had used WMDs as part of the justification to invade Iraq.

Move America Forward had little money, so it began fundraising via talk radio and e-mails. Time was short.

In an August 18 press release, MAF chairman Melanie Morgan said: "The overwhelming majority of military families support their loved ones and the missions they are serving in Iraq and Afghanistan. These military families do not share Cindy Sheehan's view of the war on terrorism, and the true story

needs to be told. We invite Americans to join us en masse in Crawford, Texas, on August 27 so we can send a message to terrorists around the world that American resolve is stronger than ever."

Talk radio and news outlets ran stories on the "You Don't Speak for Me, Cindy!" tour. Some called it a publicity stunt and criticized the motives of the groups involved. But the staff of MAF had no time to worry about the snipers in the news.

"With each day in the five days leading up to the Monday morning that we departed from San Francisco we got progressively less sleep. Five hours earlier in the week down to 1½ hours the night before when we stayed in Richmond," said Joe Wierzbicki of MAF. "After our brief catnap we affixed the banners and homemade 'You Don't Speak for Me, Cindy' sheets to our trucks and vehicles and proceeded to head towards San Francisco."

Deborah Johns, mother of a marine, was the point person for the tour. She spoke with the media about her son and the pride she has for all of America's troops. Cindy Sheehan did not speak for her.

The caravan departed from KSFO radio in San Francisco then headed to Vacaville to speak with Cindy's hometown neighbors. As it pulled off of Interstate 505, the caravan could see a sea of red, white, and blue. Signs and waving people greeted the crew who would travel days before meeting Cindy in Crawford.

"It was a great boost to us at a time when we were already beginning to fade from the lack of sleep and driving down to San Francisco and then back up and the stress of trying to stay together as a caravan and not lose anyone while traversing California's busy I-80," Wierzbicki said.

The crowd of about one hundred in Vacaville included a preacher, mothers, fathers, news media, and Blue Star families whose loved ones are serving in the war. Standing to the side of a makeshift stage was Joseph Williams, a Vacaville resident whose son, Michael, was killed in Iraq. He held a picture of his son and stood silently, as if he were holding a lone vigil for his child. His hands and body shook.

Joseph knew Cindy. They had both suffered the lonely pain that most Gold Star parents recognize. They had met several times and rode on a float together during the Dixon May Fair—the state's oldest fair—to honor their sons' sacrifices. Cindy's grief was still new at the time of the fair, which also marked her first Mother's Day without Casey. It was also before Cindy had joined John Kerry's campaign or had spent a day in Crawford. A Vietnam veteran who suffered with other vets abused upon their return from war, Joseph disagreed with Cindy. He wanted to join the caravan, but he couldn't afford the cost of travel.

Folks at the Vacaville rally pooled their money to send Joseph to Crawford. A woman also came forward and offered her frequent-flyer miles to him. Cindy's hometown determined to send its own representative to Crawford—a Gold Star parent whom many believed represented their core values more than Cindy did. Move America Forward also picked up donations and sold T-shirts in Vacaville to fund the trip.

But money did not roll into Move America Forward until the caravan had already traveled to Crawford and returned. MAF ultimately raised and spent about forty thousand dollars for the trip and expenses.

Most of the people and organizers paid their own way to Crawford, many driving their own vehicles—cars, trucks, motorcycles. A few drove motor homes.

Keeping ahead of the media is a task, but radio stations welcomed the anti-Cindy caravan as it hit each town. By the end of the first evening, the caravan was in Bakersfield. People responded in large numbers. By 2:00 a.m. the next day, more than a thousand e-mails clogged MAF's in-box.

Joe Wierzbicki dropped into a seat at a Double Tree Hotel and heard something that made him smile. "I've just about spent my last ounce of energy when I hear the TV in the lobby talking about the You Don't Speak for Me Cindy tour heading to Crawford," he recalled. "I look over and see it's CNN Headline News. We're now on the national radar and my adrenaline flows."

The media love a good fight, so they geared up for the big day. Their reports sparked something in people around the country. Some hopped on Harleys and others climbed into their RVs or old jalopies. By the time the caravan reached Los Angeles, crowds clamored to see the group who dared to question Mother Sheehan.

Antiwar crowds also showed their strength at some stops. When Deborah Johns spoke, Cindy's supporters sometimes hissed and yelled at her. At times, the protesters drowned out her speeches. But mostly people brought religious gifts, money, and words of encouragement. The divide of the country bounced around some stops, but as the caravan drew closer to Texas, the heat and the people's support magnified.

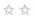

THE TRAVELERS awoke on the morning of August 27 in Dallas. They were rested and ready to roll. Mother Nature had planned a barbecue, so people packed sunscreen and umbrellas and wore hats. Texans live with the kind of heat and humidity that

would cause Satan to faint, but these folks were from all parts of the country.

They had come for all kinds of reasons. While some in the caravan were motivated to demonstrate their support for the troops, others wanted to confront Cindy and tell her the stories of their sons and daughters who died for America. Some wanted to remove crosses from a display Cindy had erected at her camp, crosses that bore the names of their fallen children. They had not given her permission to use their child's name. Many had called and left messages for Cindy to take down the crosses, but their requests were rebuffed. Later, Cindy claimed she knew nothing about the requests because she didn't respond to e-mails while she was in Crawford. (Others did that for her.)

A long stretch of cars lined up in Dallas for the last leg of the trek to Waco and then into Crawford. Families stood outside their cars and spoke about the day and why they were there. Some had lost their children, others had loved ones serving in Iraq or Afghanistan. They all had energy and expectations of getting their stories out to the world.

Steve Hayes from Tulsa, Oklahoma, drove to Texas because he'd heard enough from Cindy Sheehan. His stepson, Spc. Dustin K. McGaugh, had died in Balad, Iraq, on September 29, 2003. "This war is about not ever having another September 11 anywhere in the world," he said. To honor his son, Hayes produced a DVD about why America had to go to Iraq and Afghanistan.

The caravan pulled out of Dallas with American flags flapping from cars, trucks, motorcycles, and RVs. The line of vehicles grew longer with each mile. Big rigs and tiny cars joined. Others honked as they drove by. Every once in a while a car sporting a rainbow-colored peace sticker would pass and ges-

ture obscenely at the caravan or just ignore the red, white, and blue blur.

As the miles of vehicles approached Crawford, the local landscape included farmers standing on their land and holding up signs that read "You Don't Speak for Me, Cindy!" Some waved from their porches and fields.

CRAWFORD, TEXAS, is a town of seven hundred. But on this day, its population grew by more than four thousand. When the convoy pulled into Soldier Field, where stages had been set up for the rally, every spot of dirt road in the area was covered. A group of Harleys rumbled into town and parked under some trees for shade. Old folks in wheelchairs with flags attached, cowgirls on horses, baby carriages, long-haired teens, soldiers, West-Coast girls, Easterners flowed into the area. The field looked like a red, white, and blue sea. One horse had a message painted on its rear: "Cindy, go home!" People packed signs and posters with messages to Cindy and the world. One cowboy stood with a poster showing a silver platter holding the heads of Saddam Hussein and Osama bin Laden. A woman held a poster saying, "I lived in tyranny."

Shaded by a large white tent, people sang and spoke and listened. Jo Ann Murray Schulze played her guitar and sang "Letter Home from a Fallen Hero":

> Mother, dear Mother, how can you treat me so?
> When I died for freedom, I thought that you would know.
> I volunteered to fight for what I believe.
> Mother, dear Mother, my spirit now you grieve.

When they brought me home in honor to rest,
You met with the President and thanked him for his
 best.
Although your heart was breaking, you said that he
 was right.
Now you say America is not worth the fight.

The roll call of speakers included Gold Star parents, brothers, sisters, veterans, activists, and Deena Burnett, wife of Tom Burnett Jr., a passenger on United Flight 93 on September 11. This was the plane hijackers had hoped to plunge into either the White House or the Capitol, but the passengers had fought back, and the plane was crashed into a Pennsylvania field. Tom and Deena spoke four times by phone as the hijackers terrorized the passengers. All died in a counterattack that would be the first American act of defense in this new war. Deena spoke today with passion about her husband and the necessity of war:

We have a responsibility to our troops. Our nation stands divided. This war is not about us. We fight for those who can't fight for themselves, like my husband did. Our soldiers are doing what it takes to keep another September 11 from happening anywhere in our world. . . . Thankfully, our leaders didn't sway with public opinion and not fight. I stand in support of our troops. Our troops are promoting a better quality of life for the people in Iraq. I commend them for that and I thank them for their service to America and the world.

ACROSS TOWN at Camp Casey II, which had sprung up to handle the overflow of media handlers who had parachuted into Craw-

ford to manage Cindy's message, people came to support Cindy and her antiwar movement. The camp was crowded with all kinds of folks that day. Some had wild hair in fluorescent colors, others wore old Vietnam-era fatigues. They danced and sang old protest songs made popular by camp visitor Joan Baez, the crystalline voice of the '60s whose activist songs had helped energize protests against the war in Vietnam.

Cindy was well aware of the pro-troops folks at Soldier Field. But she did not appreciate the movement of four thousand people into Crawford: the elderly in wheelchairs, the Iraq veterans, the babies in carriages, the cowboys on horses, the Gold Star parents who did not agree with her.

While we were camping out in hot and humid Crawford, Texas, last August, trying to meet with George Bush and trying to end the war, a right-wing organization called Move America Forward (to oblivion?) started a bus tour called: Cindy, You Don't Speak for Me.

Move America Forward does some nice things, like sending coffee to our troops. It is unfortunate for the families of the almost 2,300 killed troops that the organization doesn't send non-defective GPS devices, or IED jammers to save the lives of the troops that have been put in harm's way for the politicians' lies and cowardice and corporate greed. I think these things would be a little more useful than coffee.[1]

COUNTERING
THE
PROTESTER

G ARY QUALLS WAS ALREADY in town when the pro-troops, anti-Cindy caravan pulled into Crawford. He went to meet with Cindy. They shared so much: their sons died in combat and they grieved every day. Twenty-year-old Marine Lance Cpl. Louis Qualls had died while fighting in Fallujah, about seven months after Casey's death. Beyond that horrible fissure in their bloodied souls, Gary saw nothing that would bring them together.

"What prompted me to go? I heard on the news about this lady, Cindy Sheehan," Qualls said. "I'd already lost my son. From what I saw, it was not good [what Cindy was doing]. She can't be peaceful and raising hell. I know when it's time to stand up against somebody."

Gary called Cindy and introduced himself as a Gold Star father. He expected to speak with a quiet, calm woman who was suffering from the cruelest loss of all.

"We had a nice quaint conversation. Then I asked her if I could ask her a question," Gary said. "She got real hateful. She began tapping on the phone, real belligerent and saying, 'We have a communications problem.' Then the line went dead."

Gary didn't live far from Crawford, maybe thirty minutes away. He wanted to speak with Cindy face to face, so he went to Camp Casey. He asked about their first conversation, but Cindy said she didn't remember it. They mostly talked about Casey and Louis and how they died. Gary then went with Cindy into Crawford and the Peace House, a meeting place for the antiwar, anti-Bush crowd where he hoped to tell Cindy how much she was hurting other families who'd lost loved ones in the war. When he asked her not to bring "our fallen heroes into this," Cindy "started ranting and raving."

Cindy eventually asked Gary to leave. She and the antiwar folks were going to have an important meeting, and Gary was not invited. He left the Peace House and decided he would set up his own camp in town to honor America's soldiers and call it Fort Qualls. It would be the Crawford headquarters of the movement to push back the antiwar protesters. Locals embraced Gary and helped him build Fort Qualls next to the Yellow Rose, a small shop that sells memorabilia commemorating Crawford's most famous resident, President Bush, among other Texas items. Fort Qualls's grand opening was August 27, 2005, the same day the caravan went to Crawford for its rally.

CAMP CASEY was a few miles from the president's Crawford ranch, but it might as well have been smack dab in the middle of Washington, D.C. Cindy was surrounded by media who enjoyed tables of gourmet food: sodas, sparkling water, platters of

exquisitely catered focaccia bread sandwiches, delicious finger foods, and tasty pastas—all piled high on tables under the air-cooled tent.

Back at the counterprotesters' event, local firefighters spent hours in the heat tending smoking barbecues, and the local ladies made baked beans. The firefighters did it for one of their own who had just returned from Iraq. He was angry over Cindy Sheehan's protest and what he considered to be her disloyalty to the troops.

At Cindy's tent, CBS, NBC, ABC, NPR, and CNN planted themselves in the fanned comfort that billionaire George Soros's money bought. The reporters, cameramen, and producers milled about, sampling the dessert trays.

Cindy's people had erected an entire media village (much like the Olympics). This wasn't a "small grassroots movement" that had come to Crawford to tell President Bush to bring the troops home. Miles of video cable were strewn about, attaching to a huge satellite uplink truck (which costs hundreds of thousands of dollars to rent) that was manned by professional public relations people working for Cindy.

The uplink signal was downloaded by local television stations across the country. And Cindy was sitting down for dozens of interviews that unspooled on the 6:00 news in every media market her bookers could snag.

Her people were dressed in East Coast chic: Banana Republic vests filled with notes. Toting walkie-talkies, they had cell phones plastered to their ears to direct media inquiries and schedule sit-down interviews about Cindy's demand to have a second meeting with the president.

The media were not the only ones demanding Cindy's attention. Other Gold Star parents had come to town to meet the

woman who was fast becoming the country's number-one peace activist. They wanted to tell her that they didn't agree with her. And they wanted to ask her to stop using their sons' and daughters' names in her personal war against President Bush. Only a handful of Gold Star parents sided with Cindy.

Gary Qualls was making his stand, and he would support others who disagreed with the newly anointed Peace Mom. "The media have catered to her," Gary said. "They have shown one woman. She does not speak for most of us. She's a fraud. She became a false prophet for her own organization."

14

CROSSED

I didn't want Justin's cross down there. Why would she use
my son's cross for something none of us believe in?
> —Jan Johnson on Cindy using the
> names of dead soldiers on crosses
> without family permission

J AN WATCHED EVERYTHING THAT was going on with Cindy in
Crawford and afterward. Some of Cindy's rhetoric was espe-
cially painful and personal because the two mothers had lost so
much. Their sons had been buddies and they had died so close
together. Jan thought maybe Cindy would listen to another
Gold Star mother. So she wrote her an e-mail.

"I told her who I was and about our boys," Jan said. "Then I
thought about what she was doing and I told her how I felt. I
said she was a disgrace and dishonoring her son and our boys. I
just told her."

Cindy never contacted Jan.

AMONG THE Gold Star parents who didn't want Cindy using
their children's names on the crosses erected at Camp Casey

near Crawford was Vacaville's Joseph Williams and his ex-wife, Sandy, who had come to Crawford with the caravan. They decided to walk into Cindy's camp and remove their son's name from the display.

The August heat was stifling. Back at Soldier Field, medics pumped fluids into people dried out from the blistering heat. One medic even had to hook up an IV line to himself. Joseph and Sandy staggered under the heat. Searching.

Finally, Sandy screamed. A plaintive cry. The searing knives that cut her heart on the day Michael died dug in again.

"Joseph. I found it."

She pulled the name from the cross. Tears ran across her face and dripped onto her son's name. Joseph took the piece of paper, folded it, and put it in his pocket.

"It's done now," he said.

Joseph and Sandy were not alone in culling the crosses of the names of soldiers whose families did not approve of the display. Deborah Johns did her best to collect the names of men and women whose families had asked her to remove them. One woman from Southern California suffering from cancer couldn't make the trip to Crawford. She called Deborah, who searched the displays for the name of the woman's son.

Jan didn't call anybody to remove Justin's cross. At the time, she focused on her short time with her husband before he went to war. The anguish deafened her.

"I wish I could have been able to get Justin's cross," Jan said. "It didn't belong there."

☆ ☆

MONTHS LATER, Deborah tracked down Cindy at a rally in Southern California. She had some questions. So did others.

People were losing patience with Cindy's activities, from show-ing up at the State of the Union wearing a T-shirt with the num-ber of dead soldiers emblazoned on it, to cavorting with Venezuelan president Hugo Chavez, an avowed enemy of the United States. Chavez was the first head of state to meet with Iraqi dictator Saddam Hussein after the first Gulf War.

This is a partial transcript of the confrontation:

MAN: I had a specific question with regards to the memorial you have erected in Crawford, and I believe one that you're going to be doing in Germany. You indicated that you were being supported by Gold Star . . . Gold Star Families, if I remember correctly. However, there were hundreds of military families that specifically requested that you remove their children's names from the memo-rial. However, you refused, and they actually had to come out to Crawford to remove them. When you erect memo-rials in the future, do you plan on using any names, or only names from the families that you have . . .

CINDY SHEEHAN (CS): Okay . . .

MAN: . . . received support from.

CS: My organization is Gold Star Families for Peace, and . . . and your facts aren't correct. We had a few people request that their children's names be removed, and if they re-quested, we removed their names. And . . . a memorial in Germany, I don't really . . . understand what you're talking about.

MAN: You . . . indicated . . . I believe it's the family of Derek Lee, which indicated . . . the mother e-mailed you specifi-cally, or contacted you specifically, and asked you to re-move it, and you told her to come to Crawford.

CS: No, I did not!

MAN: Are you saying that she, in fact, is not telling the truth?

CS: I didn't hear from any mother in Crawford. Number one, I didn't check any e-mail while I was in Crawford. Maybe, somebody who was checking my e-mail, you know, wrote back, but I didn't check my e-mail in Crawford. And I would never, ever, ever go against the wishes of another Gold Star mother. Ever.

DEBORAH JOHNS (DJ): Cindy, my name is Deborah Johns.

CS: Oh. Hi, Deborah. I don't speak for you!

DJ: No, you don't.

(laughter)

WOMAN: Aw, crap.

DJ: And this gentleman is absolutely correct, because it's Debbie Argel. The Williams . . . I have over 1,200 families that have sent you requests . . .

CS: Sent me requests? I'm not in charge of those memorials.

DJ: . . . California, spoke with you personally, on the telephone, and demanded that you stop using her son's name. So did Joe Williams . . .

CS: I'm not using anybody's son's name.

DJ: You have used their names in Crawford, Texas, Cindy. I was there. And I removed their sons' names. And the sheriff down there took the list of the names from me, because he said in the middle of the night, you and your people go back up and put the names back up . . .

CS: You're . . .

DJ: Cindy, you have used their names in the newspaper.

CS: You know what . . . Deborah, that's not the truth.

DJ: You have—

CS: No, I haven't used anybody's name in the newspaper.

DJ: *USA Today,* Cindy . . .

(applause)

CS: What . . . what newspaper have I used their names in?

DJ: *USA Today,* Cindy, when you—

(crosstalk)

CS: . . . I can't take that. I'm not the only person who does this stuff.

Cindy's group, Gold Star Families for Peace, and other anti-war organizations had indeed placed ads in fourteen newspapers across the nation and on cable television with the names of all of the soldiers who died in the Iraq War.

Joseph Williams had asked Cindy's group to stop using his son's name, as had others.

"So this morning, what happens? I get up and in *USA Today* . . . a full-page ad; my son's name is on it," Joseph said. "I tell you what, these people are worms."

SHEEHAN V. SHEEHAN

My husband has always agreed with me philosophically. And
he only disagreed with the intensity that I put into the fight.
—*Cindy Sheehan*[1]

I don't want Joe over there, but it's not because I don't sup-
port what's going on. I've already lost one. I don't want to
lose another. But my son died trying to give somebody else
freedom.

—*Jan Johnson on Joe's decision to
go to war, October 10, 2005*

DEATH CAN SPLINTER FAMILIES, especially when a child dies.
Grief is so personal and unique, and pain looks so differ-
ent on each mom and dad. Separation comes immediately.
Then, some recognize their spouses struggling with unbearable
pain and reach out. Some let go.

The Sheehan family was so close. Casey's death drove a
spike into their souls. The splinters were hard to put back to-
gether. His sister Carly was angry at the Bush administration.
Her blog on Myspace.com showed a picture of Carly with her
middle finger in front of her face. She said she would date a
man as long as he hated George W. Bush. Carly traveled with
her mother sometimes to protest the war. The rest of the family
was quieter about their mourning, but it burned in them.

The Johnsons drifted in and out of their narcotized exis-
tence. Anger force-fed Joe. Jan looked for light and some way to

hang on. The love between the girl who trained as a hairdresser and the soldier would stand strong. They had a tussle or two over Joe's going to Iraq. Joe realized it was selfish, but there was no other way. Every day Jan suffered. She waited for the recurring nightmare of soldiers knocking on her door. *"Ma'am. We regret to inform you . . ."*

Every time they talked on the phone, Jan told her soldier husband, "Keep your head tucked."

Joe always said, "I'll be all right. If it's my time to go, don't matter where I am."

☆ ☆

CINDY WAS in Crawford, trying to flush President Bush out, when a process server found her and handed over the lawsuit that would end her marriage. Casey's father filed for divorce on August 12, 2005, at 2:47 p.m. Pacific time. He cited irreconcilable differences.

Court papers show that Cindy and Pat separated on June 1, 2005, after twenty-eight years and two months together.

Cindy wasn't surprised when she received the divorce papers. She had a boyfriend and decided not to reconcile with Pat, even though he wanted to forgive her and fix their relationship.

Pat spoke regularly, almost daily, with his sister, Cherie. He wanted so much to put his family back together again. He told her that Cindy's grief had turned into panic attacks that forced her to leave a job with Napa County. At home, she took refuge with a computer that became her companion day and night.

"This went on for months," Cherie recounted. "Cindy had become addicted to online chat rooms of a pornographic nature. She had many men communicating with her. She eventually had physical rendezvous as well.

"Her grief may have been the cause, but at this point her marriage was in jeopardy. Pat pleaded for her to seek counseling with him; he wanted to mend the marriage, keep the family whole and help Cindy heal."

But Cindy was busy with her protests and speaking engagements, even before she became a household name in August in Crawford. Before big-money supporters came through or Cindy started charging fees for her appearances, she used most of the five hundred thousand dollars the family received when Casey died.

Only twice did she make time for counseling sessions.

"Just before she left for her road trip with the Veterans for Peace, right before Crawford, Cindy told Pat she was in love with another man and that their marriage was over," Cherie said.

When she left her Vacaville home, her family in tatters, she also left behind the evidence of her pornography addictions and her dalliances. It plunged Pat's heart into another sort of pain. His son was gone, and now his wife of twenty-eight years was gone as well.

The Sheehan divorce stretched over months. Cindy and Pat fought over the house and Casey's death benefits. Pat wanted Cindy to pay for his attorney fees and the costs of the divorce, plus spousal support. Public scrutiny heightened the pain for the couple and their adult children.

Cindy had not told her children about her affair with Lew Rockwell, a married right-winger with a libertarian bent that led him to anarchist views and to despise President Bush. Cindy regularly contributed to Lew's Web site and helped him to raise money at a special speaking event.

During the one-year anniversary of her protest in Crawford,

Texas, Cindy abruptly left the president's hometown to tell her children about this relationship. She believed news of her affair was leaking to the public, and she feared that her children would hear about her dalliances. Cindy wanted them to hear the news from her.

When she arrived in the San Francisco Bay Area, she confessed everything to her children. Family members reported that Cindy told the children that she wanted to marry Lew, but he refused to leave his wife.

A couple of days later, Cindy returned to Crawford but was hospitalized for a gynecological procedure and dehydration. Her return to Camp Casey didn't capture the attention of the media as had her initial protest in 2005.

According to family members, the Sheehan family's deterioration was punctuated by painful evidence of Cindy's liaisons in hundreds of explicit e-mails and instant messages between Lew and her.

Pat tried to get his life together. He attended church at St. Mary's, whose congregation accepted and loved him. The parishioners were protective of Pat and the Sheehans' grown children, but they were uncomfortable talking about the Sheehans' saga. Enough was enough. Casey had been a decent man, so loyal to God. St. Mary's people would be loyal to his brother and sisters and father. They would mostly be quiet about Cindy, who had brought so much unwanted examination of Vacaville and her residents.

Pat removed Casey's uniform and other items from a storage facility and began wearing the camouflage shirt to protests in Benicia and at the University of California at Davis, where daughter Carly studies. Pat's family and Cindy always had political differences, but they exploded the summer Cindy went in

Crawford. Cherie and Casey's grandparents and aunts and uncles signed a letter and sent it to Melanie Morgan about their differences. Soon, the letter spread on the Internet and popped up on Matt Drudge's Web site (www.drudgereport.com).

Dear Melanie,

Our family has been so distressed by the recent activities of Cindy we are breaking our silence and we have collectively written a statement for release. Feel free to distribute it as you wish. Thanks, Cherie

In response to questions regarding the Cindy Sheehan/Crawford Texas issue: Sheehan Family Statement:

The Sheehan Family lost our beloved Casey in the Iraq War and we have been silently, respectfully grieving. We do not agree with the political motivations and publicity tactics of Cindy Sheehan. She now appears to be promoting her own personal agenda and notoriety at the expense of her son's good name and reputation.

The rest of the Sheehan Family supports the troops, our country, and our President, silently, with prayer and respect.

Sincerely,

Casey Sheehan's grandparents, aunts,

uncles, and numerous cousins

The letter caused a firestorm of debate in the country. It also ripped a hole in the veneer of Sheehan family unity. And the reelection of George Bush had already fueled the politics of destruction in the Sheehan family.

"When they supported George Bush in November and when they voted for the man who I considered killed their grandson, that's when, that was it," Cindy said. "That to me

was a betrayal of Casey, and it hurt me so deeply. I haven't spoken to them since."[2]

☆ ☆

CINDY CONTINUED to travel and fight against what she considered an unjust and illegal war and a criminal president. Her son Andy asked her to come home, but she couldn't stop her activism. It was too much a part of her being. She was no longer Cindy Sheehan, mother and wife. Now she was Mother Sheehan, Cindy the avenger, activist Cindy Sheehan.

"Having Casey murdered in Iraq by George Bush's reckless policies has been hard enough on my family, but my setting off on my holy war to bring the troops home, my constant absences, and all of the media attention have put additional stresses on my family," Cindy wrote. "I chose my path after Casey died. The rest of the family have chosen theirs. We all still love each other and support each other in anything that we do."[3]

Pat tried rebuilding his family, a painful, grueling, and sometimes thankless goal. Everybody seemed broken beyond repair, and they mourned like strangers. Cindy took up with another man. Andy worked hard and got a tattoo on his shoulder memorializing his brother. Later, he got a tattoo of Batman; he and Casey had called each other Batman and Robin when they bowled together. Cindy had her ankle tattooed to permanently mark her body as Casey's mother. Janey, according to Cindy,[4] dealt with Casey's death by drinking and drugs. Carly sometimes traveled with Cindy. She also worked as a bartender and went to school at UC Davis. Sometimes, the family almost looked functional. Then something else would pop up.

Pat was tired of the media and all that had happened since

his family released its statement and Cindy took to hunting down President Bush.

"You just don't understand what has happened to my family because of Cindy's activism," he said. "It's just that the media has burned me so many times. I'm struggling with lots of things, keeping my adult kids together, trying to keep all of us together."

Pat wanted to stay off stage. He wanted people to remember Casey and not all of the controversy about Cindy.

Pat knows that this isn't possible, not after all that has happened. Cindy's activism has hurt his parents so deeply that they still feel that they never had a chance to grieve as grandparents. Sometimes it seemed as though Cindy were pointing at them when she lashed out at President Bush, whom they had supported. But they had suffered the loss of Casey too. For years, the grandkids had lived a couple doors down the street; they were always together, always close. Whenever they think of him, they remember Casey as a giggling toddler with knobby knees. Now he's gone and it seems to them that Cindy blames them and everybody who supports the president.

Pat wants to find a sense of normalcy, but with Cindy on the world stage as the grieving peace mother, the pain of Casey's death continues to shock him over and over again. It's like an unending horror film with his son dead and his ex-wife traveling the world with strangers and constant media coverage.

Cindy and Pat had been together since high school, best friends, and now they had lost their son and their marriage. Grief and the hungry media had consumed them.

16

MAN WITH A MISSION

I'm just praying for the last run.

—Jan Johnson on Joe's job
outside of the wire

JOE'S FAMILY SUFFERED DAILY while he fought in Iraq. Jan kept
herself going, but worry always started the day and ended it.
Sometimes sleep wouldn't come. Sometimes she wondered why
she loved Joe so much. Joe wondered the same thing. "To tell
you the truth, I don't know why she loves me," he said.

Joe and Jan didn't like each other at all when friends first in-
troduced them. But they grew on each other and then swore to
live with each other until death. In the early days, Joe was a wild
man.

"I would say back then the partying came first," Joe said. "I
mean the kids didn't go without, you know, but as far as spend-
ing time with them, I would rather be off drinking beer with
my brothers than playing with the kids, or taking them swim-
ming or stuff like that. . . . I didn't really start spending time

with them until I got back in the church—that was '95, I think, and stopped my drinking and partying."

Everything changed again when Justin died. Joe made the promise to his youngest son about revenge. He had a mission, yet he knew it wouldn't dull the ache tattooed on his heart.

Inside Iraq, Joe was motivated to complete his mission. "Hopin' to shoot somebody," he wryly mused.

By Christmas 2005, Joe was softening up on God. It wasn't easy staying angry at the Big Guy, especially for a Southerner who had been baptized more than once and who had served the Lord at home and in the mission field of Ecuador.

On Christmas morning, Jan was at home and Joe was in Iraq preparing to go on a run. His guys always prayed before they left the wire. Nobody wanted to lead prayers, so Joe volunteered. And it felt good to praise God.

Later he went on a convoy to Jordan. It was a fateful day. Joe's driver complained that his arm was hurting, so they switched places. Joe drove and the driver manned the big gun. About 3:00 p.m. a sandstorm blew up. Joe's Humvee was number six in line when an IED went off and shattered the windshield of the front vehicle. The gunner bled from his nose and ears, common concussion injuries.

Fifteen minutes later, another IED exploded and hit two trucks in front of Joe's.

"There was a lot of screaming and yelling over the radio," Joe said. "I just knew that someone had been hurt bad. Luckily, they had mild concussions. Their Humvee didn't fare so well. Holes all in it, broke the windshield, popped two tires."

The guys in the truck behind Joe's saw a couple of men running to a small pickup.

"The gunner lit them up with a .50-caliber machine gun,"

Joe said. "I don't want to sound like a warmonger, but I was disappointed that I was driving and wasn't able to shoot."

Joe figured there would be more opportunities to kill a *haji*, an Iraqi enemy. He had other problems going on. Joe had lost his appetite, so he went to see a psychiatrist for some meds to help.

"I believe he thinks my cheese has slipped off my cracker because he had me in his office for two hours, writing notes in his book," Joe said. "By the time I left there, he knew everything but my jockstrap size. He also wants to see me once a week. I don't plan on going back. I don't need him to tell me I'm crazy. I already knew that."

A couple of weeks after Christmas, the army told Joe he would get to go home for two weeks of R&R. Jan was ready. She had bought Joe a new Dodge pickup for Christmas and had built the deck the way he wanted. She also remodeled the kitchen and purchased new dining-room furniture.

Joe's extended family decided to visit the Johnson's new home in Lyerly for Joe's return.

Jan drove into Atlanta a couple of hours early. She wanted to make sure she was there for Joe. Before getting to the airport, she visited some friends at a hotel where she stripped out of her Birkenstock sandals and old T-shirt and put on some riding-style boots and a filmy aquamarine blouse. That was about as much fuss as she could manage. No makeup—just jeans and a nice blouse that Joleen had helped her to choose.

A slew of soldiers were set to come in, so the USO was busy. One by one the soldiers filtered through an area roped off for families. A roar of approval went up every time a man or woman in uniform appeared. Story after story was written that day. A young woman who'd been married to a soldier less than

a week before he shipped out to Iraq awaited her husband's return. The crowd witnessed a soldier hold his newborn son for the first time. A blanket of estrogen warmed the place and even choked men with joyous tears.

Jan waited for her man in another area. The USO brought her closer to Joe because of their special circumstances. She hid behind a human-sized plant at the airport gate. Joe walked into the clearing and looked for his wife. Jan jumped out of her hiding place.

"Hey soldier, need a ride?"

After the reunion, Joe and Jan gathered his things and walked to the parking lot. At first they didn't talk much. Jan quietly led Joe to the new Dodge she had bought. She had a magnet made for the tailgate that showed a picture of a "soldier's cross" for their son using his boots, gun, and helmet. As Joe approached the truck, he didn't admire its testosterone-bulging design but instead gently touched the magnet with his war-roughened hands. His blue eyes searched for the dimension where his son resides. Jan recognized the lost look and stood silently until Joe came back to her.

"I like it," Joe said. His eyes left the magnet and followed the lines of the truck.

Jan and Joe climbed into the vehicle and headed to the historic cemetery that is Justin's final resting place among other American warriors.

"I want to go there first thing," Joe said. "It's been, what, six months since I seen him?"

Jan was the designated driver from Atlanta to Rome, some two hours away. Returning soldiers carry war ghosts with them when they go home, even if it's for two weeks of R&R. Just driving a car is dangerous. The soldier is always on the lookout

for roadside bombs. Joe usually shoots these items with his big guns as he patrols the roads in a bullet-scarred Humvee. Dodging, shooting, and escaping are parts of defensive driving in a war zone. Back in the States, erratic driving means tickets, accidents, and even a trip to a military shrink.

WHILE HE was home, Joe finished some business. The Georgia House of Representatives voted to name a roadway after Justin. Joe and Jan went to the Capitol for the occasion.

The morning after President Bush's 2006 State of the Union Address, Cindy Sheehan and the Johnsons again made headlines. Cindy was on the front page for allegedly protesting inside the chambers of the House of Representatives. Joe and Jan were on the front page of their hometown newspaper because of the resolution promulgated by the Georgia House of Representatives.

Cindy attended the State of the Union after Bay Area Rep. Lynn Woolsey (D-CA), a liberal antiwar congresswoman, invited her. Cindy wore a T-shirt protesting the Iraq War. Police arrested her for a misdemeanor. House rules forbid activism and demonstrations. A congressman's wife was also escorted from the chambers. Later, police had to apologize to the women, saying they had not violated any rules.

In Georgia, the Johnsons were pictured in the *Rome News-Tribune* as the Georgia House unanimously passed the resolution dedicating the roadway after Justin. They too sat in the House gallery. Joe wore his Class As uniform.

JOE'S LEAVE was too short, of course. Granddaughter Jordan was almost a permanent fixture on her Da's leg, and the other

Johnsons might as well have moved in. Nobody wanted Joe back in the war zone. He was starting to want out too. Joe could see how his decision had crippled his family, and it bothered him.

"I put my desires over what my family needed," Joe said. "Personally, I think I should have stayed home with Jan. That would have been the right thing to do. But I put myself ahead of what should have been done and went ahead and went anyway."

The day he left to go back to Iraq, Jordan got out of bed early and visited her Da. She saw that he was in his uniform. It angered her, so she ignored him.

"Did Da go back to war?" Jordan later asked Jan.

"Yes, baby."

JUST US—NO PEACE

This is a society where people make money doing what they
do and I have to pay my bills, too.
> —*Cindy Sheehan on signing a*
> *contract to make money for talking*
> *about Casey's death*

CINDY WADED THROUGH HER new life with the weight of
Casey's death pushing on her. She always kept her humor
and laughed out loud, but pain was her driving force. To out-
siders, she seemed to do more and more outrageous things to
get attention. The public was less and less enamored.

By the end of summer 2005, an ABC poll showed that most
Americans knew of Cindy, but her campaign had not persuaded
many to join her crusade. In fact, she had persuaded some folks
who had been antiwar to support the war in Iraq. The poll, con-
ducted by ABC/Washington Post and released August 29, 2005,
showed that 75 percent of Americans had heard of Cindy's
protest. Her professional PR people had succeeded in getting
the message out. But she didn't gain traction with Middle
America. Her jet-setting with radical celebrities rubbed folks

the wrong way, and by New Year's 2006, Cindy's mission was slipping.

Trouble started right after her Crawford vigil, when Hurricane Katrina struck the Gulf Coast. Cindy complained that the media were giving too much camera time to the victims there. Then she decided to put herself in the center of the rescue-and-relief efforts, but nobody paid much attention.

She continued traveling the country—and Europe—protesting the war and berating Bush. But the media were distracted, so Cindy didn't get the play she enjoyed while in Crawford. The world's bad boys, such as former KKK leader David Duke and Venezuelan president Hugo Chavez praised Cindy. She denounced Duke but made worldwide headlines again by hugging Chavez during a joint event at the Sixth World Social Forum in Caracas. Earlier, she had appeared at an event with the spokesman for al Sadr, the radical Muslim leader whose troops had killed Casey.

Cindy wasn't making friends back home, but she was bringing in money. Speaking Matters LLC contracted with her to arrange for paid speeches. She could make tens of thousands of dollars to spread her antiwar message. She appeared at universities and private events around the world. She did not usually share a stage with somebody with an opposing view. The State University College at Oneonta in New York paid Cindy eleven thousand dollars for a speech in late November. In order to be fair and balanced, the university paid six hundred dollars to Lt. Col. Scott Rutter, a retired officer who led an infantry battalion in Baghdad. He spoke at noon and Cindy's event was at 8:00 p.m.

Cindy's appearances spawned protests, whether at universities or hospitals. She was a divisive figure, and the strong feelings began to affect her personal relationships.

Her old friend Mary Ferrari could no longer tolerate Cindy's behavior. "I don't know this woman who is walking around calling herself Casey's mother," Mary said. "I feel she betrayed me. In spite of everything, I still say a prayer for her every night."

Cindy admitted that she had only one friend left in the Vacaville area. Liz Kroman, her best buddy since the early '90s, was proud of Cindy. She talked to her often, and the two visited Casey's grave together whenever Cindy visited Vacaville. When Cindy called to tell Liz that actress Susan Sarandon was going to portray Cindy in a movie, Liz asked, "Who's going to play me?" The two laughed.

In early December 2005, Cindy challenged the IRS to audit her because somebody was circulating a petition to have the government look at Cindy's finances. "I have publicly said for months that I am not paying my 2004 income taxes," Cindy said on Politicalaffairs.net. "I welcome the chance to go to trial, or be audited for not paying my taxes. Then I can tell the world why: George Bush and his lying bunch of criminal neocons deceived the world into an illegal and immoral invasion of a country that was no threat to the USA. My oldest, dearest son is dead because of their lies. Give me back Casey and I'll pay your damn taxes."

Most people don't want to pay their taxes, but Cindy had already proved that she would hold hers back. The IRS had liened her and Pat for nonpayment of taxes in 1995, 1996, and 1997, according to legal documents at the Solano County Assessor Record's Office. The total bill of $23,448 was paid on September 8, 2004—five months after Casey died.

Cindy knew her peace movement was not winning the fight, though she put on her PR face and told true believers that

they had a foothold. In April 2006, a friend, Scott Ritter, a leading war critic who was a retired marine and weapons inspector leading up to the war, decried that no peace movement exists.

First of all, what is the peace movement? There is no national peace movement. There's a conglomeration of organizations, all of which are ego-driven. If you take a look at Peace Action, they have a national Peace Action and they have state Peace Actions around the country. They don't work well with each other; they don't get along with each other. They feud. They don't have a centralized plan.

You have Cindy Sheehan running around, a symbol of the peace movement. A symbol of what? Who is she? Who nominated her to be the spokesperson? She did one brave thing. I'm all for what Cindy Sheehan did last August. But people say, "She sacrificed so much." She didn't sacrifice anything. Her son sacrificed his life. In order for Cindy Sheehan to have sacrificed anything, she would have to have given up her son to the military. The last time I checked, he was an adult. He signed a contract. He went into the military. He went off to war, and he died. And, yes, it's a tragedy that he died, and it's a bigger tragedy that he died in a war that I believe is an illegal war of aggression. There should not have been a war to begin with. But Cindy Sheehan didn't sacrifice a damn thing; her son did. He made the ultimate sacrifice in service to this country. That's a tragedy that he died.

But this is the problem with the antiwar movement—they lionize people for artificial reasons. They give them artificial standing. There's no depth to it. There's no direction. Where does the peace movement want to go? Cindy Sheehan, in her own response to my [recent] article [criticizing the antiwar movement], spoke of defending a woman's reproductive rights. You know

what, Cindy? Go do that. But don't call yourself the peace movement when you do that. Because when you do that, all you do is basically take the energy that's necessary to have a genuine peace movement, to have a true impact, and you allow that to basically just be spread and wasted. It's wasted energy. There is no peace movement. There is no peace movement. It's a bunch of people who claim they're part of a peace movement, but there is no peace movement.

I'm a football fan. At the end of the day, I judge a coach and a team by the score that exists on the scoreboard when the end of the fourth quarter comes. And right now, it's the pro-war movement 60, the antiwar movement nothing. Someone can't tell me, "No, no, we're doing OK." No, you're not. You're getting beat, and you need to recognize you're getting beat, and you need to figure out why you're getting beat, and you need to figure out what you need to do to get yourself back on track. And the key thing here is: Bring a sense of focus and organization, which is lacking.[1]

Cindy recognized that her beloved peace movement suffered bad PR and anemic energy. But that could and should change, she wrote.

The antiwar movement is not on the "verge of collapse" because we are not organized, or because we don't take a "warrior's" view of attacking the neocons and the war machine using the tactics of Napoleon, or Sun Tzu—but because the two-thirds of Americans who philosophically agree that the war is wrong, BushCo lied, and the troops should come home, will not get off of their collective, complacent, and comfortable behinds to demonstrate their dissent with our government.

187

The challenge of the peace movement, now that we have
identified the problem so well, and have the vast majority of
Americans on our side, is to convince each and every last
American that he/she has a very intimate and personal stake in
what we are allowing our government to do in Iraq and the
world.[2]

By April 2006, Cindy's campaign had taken some hard hits
from all sides. Most painful were the negative words from Scott
Ritter, a political friend. Cindy was lonely. It's hard to spend
time with loved ones when you're traveling the world with little
time at home.

In the first week of April 2006, the Revolution Youth Group
of San Francisco's Lowell High School invited Cindy to speak to
a school assembly. Cindy showed up to the school in her
brand-new convertible Volkswagen. Police had reserved a spot
in front of the school for her and cordoned off a full block on
the other side of the street so nobody could park near Cindy.
The police presence looked like security for a head of state.

Cindy was escorted to the gym where she sat cross-legged,
sipping bottled water, on the stage. The gym was stuffed to the
rafters, but Cindy was relaxed. She spoke for about thirty-five
minutes then took questions. It was here that she talked about a
change in her mantra, a softening of her position to "get the
troops out now!"

The crowd was Cindy-friendly, hooraying when Cindy
hammered home her points. Yet something happened when she
took questions. Most students said they were liberal and anti-
war, but they did not like some of her behavior, such as hang-
ing out with Hugo Chavez. When a student asked what might
happen if we immediately pulled out American troops, as she

wished, Cindy made a remarkable statement. She had always demanded a complete withdrawal of troops.

"I'm not naive enough to know that we can bring them all home today," she said. "We have to start a gradual drawdown of the shooting coalition troops and we need to replace the shooting troops with an army of diplomats with a Middle Eastern face on them."

Bruised by critics from her own camp and recognizing the soft spots in her battle plan, Cindy had changed. She left the auditorium to little fanfare. About fifty people stood across the street holding pictures of their children, flags, and signs to protest Cindy's presence.

Cindy got into her Volkswagen and drove past them. She put her arm out the window and flashed a peace sign.

THE PATRIOT

I leave out at 4.30 to go out on my first convoy here. I will be
gunning on a 5-ton truck which ain't so bad. The gunners
here remain seated until there is something to shoot at.

—*Joe Johnson in a November 9, 2005,*
e-mail to his friends and family

JOE WAS TIRED OF sitting around the barracks. The action was
outside the wire. Time passed like death when he wasn't part
of a convoy. He lived for the adrenaline. If he needed to kill
somebody, Joe would gladly pull the trigger.

"I don't think I'm going to lose any sleep over it. And I
know that sounds bad, but especially if you know for sure that
they've been settin' bombs on the side of the road, I won't feel
bad at all, I don't think," he said. "I mean that's easy to say be-
cause I hadn't killed anybody yet, but there's several people in
my section that has and they don't seem like it bothers them
any, you know. And the guy that shot at the trigger man a few
weeks ago on Christmas Day, I asked him how he felt about
probably killing somebody and he said, 'I'm okay with it.'"

Joe knew that, no matter what happened in Iraq, he wouldn't

be satisfied that he left a mark for Justin. Every day that he held the machine gun and searched the roads for bombs and killers, he thought of his son. He was angry but tired.

"I could kill all the insurgents and it would never bring Justin back," he said. "I don't think I'll really get anything out of it except for maybe that one moment of satisfaction when I finally kill somebody. But as far as long-lasting feelings of satisfaction, I don't think I'll find it in Iraq. There's hardly a day goes by that I don't wish I hadn't a spent more time with him."

In Iraq, he spent every day thinking about Justin. About the curly headed little boy and the wild teen. About the two of them working together and fighting over something stupid. About how Joe had not been in Iraq to protect his son.

Some days Joe wondered if he could ever go back to his life as a homebuilder. The work could get boring. After shooting at bad guys and living through bombs and shootings, nothing feels exciting. He considered returning to Iraq to drive trucks as a civilian. The money was good, and it kept the heart pumping. The only problem is that truck drivers can't have guns; that's what the military escorts are for. But Joe liked having a gun on him. A guy would have to get too close to kill him with a knife. Maybe he would be a contract killer. A mercenary aiming for terrorists. No. None of these things would work. They'd hurt Jan. He had to stop thinking of his own pain and look after his family.

Jan saved enough money for the couple to buy a fixer-upper house so they could work on it together. They always enjoyed that kind of job. The two of them together, hammering boards and putting on shingles. When the house was all fixed up, they could sell it and make some money. Then roll the cash into another house.

Joe's grandbabies waited for Da to come home. Jordan

planned to take him and run away with him. Or at least go down to the "campsite" on the property. It has a little sand beach where she and Da could hang out and nobody could bother them and there would be no war. The war took Justin. It hurt and she missed him. She even made him a Valentine on February 14, 2006, and gave it to Gannie. "This is for Justin. Keep it till you see him again," Jordan said.

Jan wanted so much to spend summer nights with Joe and the kids. They could swim in the pool and relax in the hot tub. Then the babies could climb into bed and sleep with them. Everybody would be safe.

The days with Joe outside the wire had worked her last nerve. She had built the deck, remodeled the kitchen, and helped everybody who needed help. She sewed a prom dress for a high-school gal and even worked on a big taffeta dress for herself. She would wear it for an Eastern Star function like a good southern belle. Nothing would make her feel pretty but Joe.

She needed him home. Life was passing. She always thought they'd spend every day together. Grow old. Love their grandkids. Joe was missing so much, things they should have shared, like a memorial for Justin and Casey and others from Fort Hood.

Fort Hood in April 2006 unveiled its stunning memorial for the soldiers who died in the war on terror. Jan drove Joe's pickup to Texas and met with others who lived with the same heartache. Joleen and little Justine made the trip with her. She talked to others in the unfortunate club of American mourners and missed Joe more. Jan is strong, but she needed her best buddy.

Walking along the wall of names, which looks a bit like the Vietnam memorial in Washington, D.C., Jan stopped at Justin's name. Her fingers traced the *J* and every letter in his name. *God, help me.*

She was there on April 10, 2006, the second anniversary of Justin's death. Joe should have been there. Nobody else knows the shards of broken life that pierce the soul like a spouse. The man who lost so much.

In the meantime, Joe was set to go out on another run, but his sergeant told him to stay at the base. They didn't want to screw with fate. Instead of shooting at the two-legged rats in the desert, Joe called a florist and sent a dozen roses to his wife. They looked just like the roses that lay next to Justin in his casket. Joe called a couple times that day. That helped Jan some.

She celebrated Justin's new life in another way, with a second tattoo: a red, white, and blue heart on her back for Justin. Artists tattooed Jan, Joe, and Joleen with various pieces honoring Justin. A little pain and permanent markings made sense for the man they missed too much.

Jan's phone has caller ID, so she usually knows who's calling. Some numbers come up "private," so she has to decide whether to pick up. With Joe gone, she likes to take all phone calls. You never know. Bad news can come through the phone lines, but the worst news would come in the form of an army vehicle carrying soldiers dressed in their Class A uniforms.

Bad news came. Jan's niece called. Jan's brother Bob had cancer and possibly needed a bone-marrow transplant. Jan was the closest relative. She said she'd get the tests.

"I wasn't going to look into his grandkids' eyes some day and have to tell them, 'I could have saved your granddaddy, but I didn't,'" Jan said.

If Jan were a match for her only sibling, she would have to undergo procedures that could endanger her own life. She told

Joe about her decision, and he went ballistic, cursing like a madman.

She went to the hospital and had her blood drawn. Jan figured that, sometimes, a spouse has to do something that might bother her partner. Joe did that when he went to Iraq.

SPRING IN Iraq brings dust storms that bear down on towns like tornadoes in Kansas. The wall of rage ravages vehicles, clogs guns, and sickens people. Soldiers are always cleaning their M-16s. The warming weather also inspires the crazies whose favorite sport is killing infidels—those who don't practice Islam.

Joe and his guys could feel the change in aggression. The base was targeted more and more by rocket-propelled grenades and other weapons. The road between Al Asad and Jordan was wicked. Killers prowled the route and planted IEDs for the convoys. Driving the road was like walking through minefields in Vietnam: You never know when they're going to blow or if you'll survive when they do.

Joe's group was driving when another Humvee approached a dead lamb on the road. Embedded in the rotting flesh was a bomb. It detonated. But the timing was off for the terrorists, and the explosion didn't kill anybody or disable vehicles.

An hour later, Joe came up on two cars parked to the side of the road. Joe was gunning so he had a good look at four Middle Eastern men inside the cars.

"They looked real shady, so I told the two guys with me that we should search them. We got the okay and went back. You would not believe the stuff we found on them. One guy had twelve hundred dollars in American money; we found two cell phones they use to set off bombs; also supplies to build

detonators," Joe said. "All four tested positive for explosives on their hands. I wanted to shoot them."

Joe exploded. "You dirty m—. You pieces of s— are the kind of s— that killed my boy. I should blow your f— heads off right here. You are nothing but scum. You don't deserve to live. You don't. I should f— shoot you in the heads. I can do it, you know. I can kill you right now."

He was in their faces, his spit hitting them as he cursed. His M-16 was ready to fire. Bam. Gone.

Joe's insides twitched and hurt. Rage poured out of him like he had unleashed the gates of hell. The other soldiers watched as Joe went off. They knew his story. Justin. *He's the crazy old man who came here to kick ass. This is his time. Do it.*

As fast as the rage erupted, calm brushed Joe. He stepped away.

The soldiers cuffed the men, and one had to ride with Joe in his Humvee and hear some more of Joe's philosophy of dirtbags who kill heroes like Justin.

They took the four bomb makers to Abu Ghraib prison.

JOE CAME to grips with the fact that he didn't kill when he had the chance. Maybe he wouldn't get another chance. But that's okay. He went to battle for his country. And Justin. Joe did his job.

"I put Jan and my family through hell by coming here. I'm glad it's almost over, but I hate the fact that I didn't take some of these killers out," Joe said. "I'm kind of nervous about coming home. That will end a chapter of my life and be the beginning of another one. Sometimes I don't do changes well. I guess you could say I'm a creature of habit."

Joe returned from war on May 5, 2006, and spent some time

in Savannah, Georgia, for the military to debrief him and other soldiers and check them for injuries, physical as well as mental. A soldier always thinks about coming home, but the transition is tough. Simple things like driving a car are complicated by a reflex to drive as if still in a Humvee dodging IEDs. Jan hung out in Savannah with Joe until he was ready to go home to his daughter and to his grandchildren on May 12.

Joe didn't go back to work for about six weeks because he had a lot of time to make up with his granddaughters—and Jan.

"During his 'vacation' he spent a lot of time bonding with the girls again, especially Justine," Jan said. "We didn't think she would have much to do with him, but she went straight to him as soon as he walked through the door. This lasted about two weeks, then she became my girl again."

Things got back to normal, kind of. When one of the family is gone forever, there is no going back to the way it was. And living in a war zone tweaks a guy's personality.

"Joe has trouble dealing with crowds and a lot of noise," Jan observed.

The family continues to mourn. The pain is always there, jabbing the soul between the breaths of daily realities.

"Joe is still handling his mourning about the same. He gets through, thanks to Budweiser," Jan said.

The state of Georgia dedicated an intersection to Justin on July 7, 2006. People from around the state showed up to honor the soldier from Floyd County. A guard of motorcycle riders who travel around protecting grieving families from war protesters showed up in strength.

"There were 140 Patriot Guard Riders. I nearly cried when they were led in by the state patrol," Joe said. "Had a Blackhawk helo flyover also and the fire department bagpipe team."

Joe keeps in touch with some war buddies, including a couple who joined his unit just so they could go to war and protect the country. Sometimes Joe talks about going back to Iraq with a civilian company. Before he came home, he considered working as a mercenary or a civilian truck driver. Jan prays that he's just talking. For now, the family is together, doing little things like gathering at Jordan's T-ball games and hanging out with friends.

Jordan recently gave Joe a set of screwdrivers she found at a flea market.

"She just told him he can use them with Justin when he comes home and they go back to work together," Jan said. "It makes it rough when stuff like that happens. It really brings home the fact that Justin is gone for good."

CONCLUSION

A PARENT SHOULD NEVER have to bury a child. Such a thing is unnatural. When it happens, mothers and fathers suffer overwhelming pain and guilt and sometimes anger at their departed sons and daughters. Nothing can console them. Even those with strong ties to God carry an unbearable weight that steals their breath and numbs their heart. It is easy to lash out at God. *"Why have you done this? I hate you!"*

When he heard that terrorists had killed his son, Joe Johnson turned against God and allowed his brewing emotions to ferment into white-hot hate. Hate for Muslims. Hate for religion. Even hate for himself.

After her son's death, Cindy Sheehan's hate ramped up while the initial pain and numbness died down. She already had problems with Catholicism, though she allowed the church to perform Casey's Mass of Resurrection. Her world turned inside out. An underlying bitterness toward men, a theme that jogged in and out of her life as a form of feminism, helped to poison her marriage. At one point, while she was still in shock over her son's death, Cindy ordered all men out of her house, including her husband, so her girlfriends could drink and mourn and console. But that act cut like a sword through the souls of the Sheehan men, severing them from her.

"During the time after Casey's death, [Pat and I] would speak of Cindy and her grief, their marriage, and how he could reach her and help her heal," said Cherie Quartarolo, Pat's sister and Casey's godmother. "Pat must have been more than a

little conflicted, but he is very close to all the Sheehans. We are a normal family. We all offered our help in their time of grief. Cindy, however, was resistant and made everything political, separating herself from the family."

The mourning brought out the worst in Cindy and Joe as their spouses suffered their own life-changing grief. Pat and Jan had lost their sons too, but they were abandoned at home to pick up the shattered lives of their surviving children and to heal themselves. Every day Pat tried to pull his family back together, and every day Jan held down the home front while Joe chased his demons.

Joe and Cindy wanted revenge. They lashed out at the people they believed had stolen their sons' lives. For Cindy that was President Bush. Joe blamed Muslims and later focused his anger on the terrorists in Iraq. Joe and Cindy's extreme reactions pumped themselves with enough adrenaline to allow them to briefly and sporadically forget their pain. But when they were at rest, the heartache would sneak back and remind them of the reality that had darkened their lives, the reality from which they most wanted to hide. Neither could run fast enough nor yell loud enough to fill the cavernous loss within.

"I knew Joe would never heal unless he went to Iraq, and I wondered what things would be like for us when he got back," Jan said.

At the same time, Joe worried about his returning from Iraq. He doesn't adapt well to change, and Justin's death was as big a change as any parent could suffer. In Iraq he could handle his grief by searching for the monsters who kill boys like Justin. At home he would have time to think, to ponder, to ache. Slow times. That scared him. His consolation was that he knew his wife would be there to hold him or to talk and listen.

Pat didn't have that. The love of his life had left him for another man and a life of high-profile protesting. Cindy flew around the world; her obsession devoured her. Even when she was in the media limelight, aching for Casey, she found brief moments in which she could laugh or cry at the smallest things.

The Sheehans' divorce was final at the end of June 2006, a victim of Cindy's extreme mourning. Pat kept the house in Vacaville, which is just down the street from St. Mary's Catholic Church, whose parishioners love him and his children. Andy and Janey still live with him. Carly attends the University of California at Davis. They all miss Cindy. The children have pleaded with her to come home. Their mourning is a part of their lives, a kind of normal for a family whose firstborn died so suddenly. But it is a mourning that cannot heal, because Cindy will do nothing to allow her grief to progress toward healing or coping.

In July 2006, Cindy purchased a piece of property in Crawford, Texas, about seven miles from President Bush's home. It is to be an anchor for protests against the president. She claimed that she used Casey's insurance money to buy the land, but last year she indicated that she was running out of insurance money and had to charge for her speeches to stay afloat financially.[1]

Cindy's popularity among mainstream Americans has never been higher. But a year after she and her media consultants made their stand in Crawford, her relevance has plummeted, according to Steve Janke, a blogger at www.stevejanke.com who closely follows Cindy.

"I did do a piece recently on her blog, which averages five hits a day. Five?! Well, on the day I mentioned it, traffic shot up to more than three hundred, maybe more, but [it] seems to

have returned to as close to nothing as you can get," Janke said on July 30, 2006. "That was the perfect metaphor. The media might still be chasing her, but the public, when given the choice, are ignoring her."

Cindy is still running from her grief, and her grief has a death grip on her soul. After Casey died, she yelled over and over again, "I don't want to live without my Casey." Her life without her son leaves her with two options: keep running or stay still and face the reality that her family still endures. For now, though, she has chosen to continue running.

While Cindy moved away from her family and her marriage, Joe returned home from Iraq to Jan and the mourning he left behind for a higher-octane grief punctuated by his own life-and-death daily experiences.

Joe's old ghosts returned when Justin died. He started drinking again. That continued even after he returned home to Jan, who loves him unconditionally. They share so much together, and as much as it hurt, Justin's untimely death did not fracture their marriage. They knew and shared each other's pain, a wrinkle in their life they could not erase. Time in Iraq didn't take it away from Joe. At home, Jan stood beneath the shower of fire and survived, a minute at a time. That's the way it is for parents whose children are gone forever.

Yet the veil of mourning reaches beyond parents. Aunts and uncles, grandmas and grandpas, sisters and brothers, and fellow soldiers all survive with the mountain of grief that erupts from the deepest recesses of their being until it exposes itself in wild crying or silence.

Every person mentioned in this book has walked in the shadows of grief that shocked their souls when they heard that Casey or Justin died. They are all Americans mourning. They

look for ways to express themselves or forget what they suffered. Some resort to alcohol, some choose activism.

Returning veterans from Iraq avoid standing at windows that might have meant their deaths in the war zone. The backfire of a car can send a soldier scurrying under his bed in the dead of night. The nightmare of living and dying for others soaks the sheets under which they try to sleep. The daytime turns black with memories. But when they get together, they're family. Sometimes they talk. Sometimes the silence talks for them. Nobody else understands. They are a family whose bonds are seared deeper than blood.

When veterans from Iraq could, they shared their stories with us for this book. For Casey's and Justin's lives—and the lives of every man and woman who fell—we offer this book. It is nothing when compared to all they have given us. For the survivors, we offer our prayers and our eternal thanks for bearing such a burden for a mostly grateful nation.

LUKE HERBST signed up for the National Guard after he left the army in October 2005 and spent about a month in college. He missed the military routine. The guard called him up for active duty and stationed him at Camp Navistar on the Iraq-Kuwait border on July 21, 2006. The guard also promoted him to sergeant; after his last tour, he had left Iraq as a specialist.

After terrorists killed Justin, Luke became a sniper. He doesn't like to talk about his missions.

"People always want to know if you've killed someone or did your buddies die," Luke said. "It's like *Groundhog Day*, the movie, because you get sick of telling the same thing over and over again. The only time I really talk about it is when I'm with other guys that I served with, because they're the only ones

who really know [what it's like over there] and will ever know. So a lot of people think I've told them what it was like, but I didn't tell them even a tenth [of what it's like]."

Now he's back in the war zone as a sniper. Luke also works on the security details for supply convoys. After only three days in Kuwait, Luke again suffered a blow to his heart. On his first security mission, a soldier from the 121st Field Artillery, Army National Guard was killed and two were wounded.

"He wants to do his job, and he's an asset since because of his training at Fort Hood," said Annette Meyer, Luke's mother. "I believe that Luke will be a source of comfort to the men in his unit."

Annette has struggled to help Luke, who every day still mourns the loss of Justin. Before Luke left for a yearlong stint in the war zone, he and his mother spoke about the possibility of his death.

"On June 18, Luke and I were saying good-bye before he left for Kuwait. We shared our thoughts, and I said, 'If I don't see you again, I will see you in heaven.' He answered, 'Yes, Mom.'"

DEBORAH JOHNS is working in financial management and lives near Roseville, California. She briefly flirted with the idea of running for the U.S. Senate when Cindy Sheehan announced her interest in the seat now held by Sen. Dianne Feinstein. She continues to join others in the organization she founded, Marine Moms of Northern California, making care packages for the troops overseas and counseling returning war veterans. Her son William has returned to Iraq for his third tour of duty.

PAT KNIESLER can be found every Thursday night at the antiwar vigils she organized in the small town of Benicia, California, a

forty-minute drive from San Francisco. Passersby give her both cheers and jeers. She has launched a Web site called Iraq Casualty Count and spends her time responding to it.

Father MIKE MCFADDEN continues his work in restoring traditional Catholic values at St. Mary's Church in Vacaville. He recently brought back the Latin Mass each quarter and is busy erecting two new angels on each side of the altar, hovering beside Mary and Joseph. His parishioners are delighted.

KEITH NIMLO now lives in Southern California. After he left Iraq and the army, he joined the National Guard. He could face another round in Iraq, but he said he never wants to return. Keith hopes to one day visit the Johnsons in Georgia. Justin's memory—his laughter, great humor, their last moments together—is with him every day.

GARY QUALLS is on disability for his heroic twenty-eight-year career in the military, but he is not disengaged from the political wars that surround Crawford, Texas. He keeps an eye on the Peace House funded by the left-wing factions who purchased it in anticipation of making the president's ranch home ground zero for antiwar activities. Qualls volunteers his time for an organization for Gold Star Families headed by State Representative Chuck Larson of Iowa.

He is also working to change his status as underground bachelor in the county.

PAT SHEEHAN lives in Vacaville, California, where he and some of his adult children attend church at St. Mary's Church. He is not far from the cemetery where his hero son lies among other

war veterans, city leaders and everyday people. Lately, he has taken to wearing Casey's camouflage uniform and has joined antiwar activities in and around his town. Pat hopes to heal the rift amidst his relatives brought on by his wife's words and actions. He aims to live up to the ideals of his son, who is his hero.

JOSEPH WILLIAMS AND SANDY WATSON Joseph owns a hair-styling salon, Chocolate City, in Fairfield, California, not far from the Sheehan family. He spends his time listening to talk radio, and making public appearances to counter Cindy Sheehan's activism. Sandy has re-married and lives quietly in Phoenix, Arizona, satisfied that she found her son's name attached to a roadside cross the antiwar crowd in Crawford, Texas, constructed. Sandy brought the slip of paper back home.

JOE WIERZBICKI remains the senior strategist for Move America Forward. He is currently working on arranging a trip to Iraq for Gold Star family members who wish to visit the country in which their sons and daughters died to see for themselves that their children's sacrifice was not in vain.

ACKNOWLEDGMENTS
NOTES
INDEX

ACKNOWLEDGMENTS

Without the help of Joe and Jan Johnson, their friends and family—daughter Joleen and son Joshua—and the soldiers who knew both Casey Sheehan and Justin Johnson, this book would not have been possible. Levi Lohnes, Keith Nimlo, and Luke Herbst are true heroes who served in Iraq then selflessly told their stories. They have shared the most intimate details of their lives and trusted us to tell their stories as accurately as possible.

We were blessed with the cooperation of a brave woman, Cherie Quartarolo, Casey's aunt and godmother. All of Casey's paternal family have suffered silently and mourned with dignity. We pray for their peace.

We are grateful to Joseph Williams, who lost his son, Michael, in Iraq in the first days of the war; Shawn and John Wroblewski; Gary Qualls; Von and Diane Ibbotson; Mark Crowley; Deborah Tainsh; Deb Argel-Bastien; Annette Meyer; and other Gold Star Family members we've met along the way.

We offer deep thanks to the families of the wounded and our veterans of all wars who suffered and still suffer from the pain experienced during their service.

Special thanks to Deborah Johns, mother of Marine Cpl. William Johns, for her unstinting efforts to tell the truth about the war in Iraq.

We are deeply appreciative of the support and encouragement we've received from our own families, especially our noisy, demanding, but loving teenagers Mandi and C.J., and from sister Annette, who edited with an accountant's eye and as a lover

of good books. Most especially we thank our husbands, Ken Moy and Jack Swanson, who willingly picked up the reins of responsibility while we traveled and worked on the writing of this story. Uncle Howard too.

Thanks also to:

- KSFO Radio in San Francisco, whose management allowed us to meet and become friends and partners on this project.
- Lee Rodgers, Tom Benner, and Brian Sussman, as well as überproducer Sheri Yee.
- The *Vacaville Reporter* in Vacaville, California.
- Ron Pitkin, who took a chance on us, and all of the folks at Cumberland House who worked on this project.
- Buzz Patterson for his support.
- Sean Hannity and David Limbaugh for their kind hearts and encouragement.
- Kristen Schremp of KAS Publicity LLC who lead us through the complicated "new world" of publicizing a book project.
- EDitor, also known as Ed Curtis, who painstakingly EDited this story with the patience of a saint.

We can't forget all of the good people of Vacaville who stood strong during the glaring spotlight as people around the world probed the small town where heroes are born. Thank you Mayor Len Augustine and Vice Mayor Pauline Clancy, strong leaders with true compassion and love for our troops.

We owe the deepest debt of gratitude to the men and women of the U.S. military who serve willingly and with honor and distinction in order that our lives are safer, better, and uphold the standards upon which this great nation was founded.

NOTES

CHAPTER 1: HOLY WEEK

1. Cindy Sheehan, *Not One More Mother's Child* (Kihei, HI: Koa Books, 2005), 7.

2. Cindy Sheehan, "Maverick of the Year," www.rollingstone.com /news/story/8957186/cindy_sheehan.

3. Stacy Bannerman, "Spiritual Activism in the Time of War," November 2005. http://edgelife.net/article.php?id=0077.

4. Pat Sheehan, interview and documentary by Theo Rigby, www.theoriby.com.

5. Cindy Sheehan, interview with Daily Kos, August 1, 2005, http://darksyde.dailykos.com/story/2005/8/1/2161/52638.

6. Cindy Sheehan, "The Sounds of Hope," reprinted in *Not One More Mother's Child*, 35–36.

7. Sheehan, interview with Daily Kos, August 1, 2005, http:// darksyde.dailykos.com/story/2005/8/1/2161/52638.

CHAPTER 2: JUSTIN'S DECISION

1. Cindy Sheehan, Address to Veterans for Peace Convention, August 5, 2005.

2. See North Rome Church of God, http://www.nrcog.org/about .html.

CHAPTER 3: AMERICAN SOLDIERS

1. Cindy Sheehan, *Not One More Mother's Child* (Kihei, HI: Koa Books, 2005), 9.

2. Chris Conley, "Cloudland Canyon Hosts Rescue Training," February 23, 2000, http://www.dadesentinel.com/22300–1.htm.

3. Associated Press. "Most Americans Not Fit to Serve," March 13, 2006, http://www.military.com/NewsContent/0,13319,90736,00.html?ESRC=army.nl.

4. Cindy Sheehan, Speech at the Congressional Forum on the Downing Street Memo, Washington DC, June 16, 2005.

5. Sheehan, *Not One More Mother's Child*, 7–8.

6. Ibid., 6.

7. Mark Poblete, http://www.fallenheroesmemorial.com/oif/profiles/sheehancasey.html.

8. "Origins of the Chaplaincy," U.S. Army History, http://www.usachcs.army.mil/history/brief/chapter_1.htm.

9. Not her real name.

10. Casey Sheehan was registered in Solano County, where documents show his party affiliation and voting record.

11. Darksyde, "Interview with Gold Star Mother, Cindy Sheehan," *Daily Kos*, August 1, 2005, http://darksyde.dailykos.com/story/2005/8/2161/52638.

12. Carly Sheehan, quoted in an Associated Press article after her brother's funeral, April 14, 2004.

CHAPTER 5: SIX DAYS IN SADR

1. Cindy Sheehan, *Not One More Mother's Child* (Kihei, HI: Koa Books, 2005), 101. Cindy allegedly made this statement in an e-mail to television producers. She has since denied making the statement and accused a former friend of altering the e-mail. He and another witness claim Cindy made the statement.

2. Information for the fight in Sadr City comes from eyewitness accounts and historical and military sources.

3. http://familiesunitedmission.com/docs/families/midwest/ibbotson.shtml.

4. U.S. Department of Defense, news release no. 273–04, April 7,

2004, http://www.defenselink.mil/releases/2004/nr20040407–0531 .html.

CHAPTER 6: DAY SIX

1. Levi Lohnes published this blog while he was in Iraq. It later appeared in *People* magazine. He edited it for this book.

CHAPTER 7: SOULS ON FIRE

1. Rome, Georgia, official Web site, "Myrtle Hill: One of Rome's Seven," http://www.romegeorgia.com/myrtleh1.html.

2. Cindy Sheehan, "A Markerless Grave," April 11, 2006, http://www.truthout.org/docs_2006/041106Z.shtml.

3. Cindy Sheehan, *Not One More Mother's Child* (Kihei, HI: Koa Books, 2005), 7.

CHAPTER 8: THE MINISTERS

1. Cindy Sheehan, blog, DailyKos.com, August 1, 2005.

2. Diane Wagner, "It's Harder to Bear Now," *Rome News-Tribune*, March 27, 2005.

3. Fallen Heroes Memorial, http://www.fallenheroesmemorial .com/oif/profiles/sheehancasey.html.

4. Cindy Sheehan, *Not One More Mother's Child* (Kihei, HI: Koa Books, 2005), 7.

CHAPTER 10: CAMP CASEY

1. Cindy Sheehan, from a rally and speech, Camp Casey II, Crawford, Texas, August 27, 2005.

2. Cindy Sheehan, *Not One More Mother's Child* (Kihei, HI: Koa Books, 2005), 193.

3. Ronan Sheehan, "Cindy Sheehan's Irish Interview: Sheehan to

Sheehan," Counterpunch, January 10, 2006, http://www.counterpunch .org/sheehan01102006.html.

4. "Real Voices Kickoff," July 31, 2004, http://www.angelfire.com /sk3/spkhntrca/Casey.html.

5. David Kravets, "California Justices Skirt Voter Privacy Issues Until After Election," NCTimes.com, October 18, 2004, http://www .nctimes.com/articles/2004/10/20/election2004/state/18_18_5010_18 _04.txt.

6. Joshua Franks, "Cindy Sheehan and Lesser Evil Politics," Znet, February 3, 2006, http://www.zmag.org/content/showarticle.cfm? ItemID=9649.

7. Sheehan, *Not One More Mother's Child,* 74.

8. David Henson, "Bush, Sheehans Share Moments," *Vacaville Reporter,* June 24, 2004.

9. "Drudge Getting Roved?" DailyKos.com; Neoeconomist, August 11, 2005, http://www.dailykos.com/story/2005/8/11/154713/896.

10. August 11, 2001, http://www.attytood.com/archives/002306 .html.

11. Cindy Sheehan, "Day Five: The Truth Scares People," August 10, 2005, www.michaelmoore.com/mustread/index.php?id=452.

12. Byron York, "Cindy Sheehan's Radical Strategist," National Review Online, August 29, 2006, www.nationalreview.com/york/york /200508290901.asp.

13. Jennifer Verner, "America's Red Army," FrontPageMagazine.com, September 1, 2004, http://frontpagemag.com/articles/readarticle.asp? ID=14893.

CHAPTER 11: MEDIA GONE WILD

1. Cindy Sheehan, "OutFOXed?" October 26, 2005, http://www .huffingtonpost.com/cindy-sheehan/outfoxed_b_9594.html.

2. Cindy Sheehan, "Day 3 of the Peace Occupation of Crawford,"

August 8, 2005, http://www.dailykos.com/story/2005/8/9/01024/39519.

3. Christopher Hitchens, "Cindy Sheehan's Sinister Piffle: What's Wrong with Her Crawford Protest," August 15, 2005, http://www.slate.com/id/2124500/.

4. "Cindy Sheehan Leaves NPR Liberal Speechless," August 30, 2005, http://freerepublic.info/focus/f-news/1473423/posts?page=264.

5. Sheehan, "OutFOXed?"

6. Ibid.

7. Editorial, "Polarized Views," *Vacaville Reporter,* August 15, 2005.

8. The two August 28, 2005, photographs of Sheehan and Sharpton can be seen online at http://www.littlegreenfootballs.com/weblog/?entry=17266_How_Phony_Can_They_Get&only.

9. "Fonda Won't Protest War," April 18, 2006, Associated Press.

10. Howie Klein, "Meeting Cindy Sheehan," Advocate.Com, September 8, 2005.

11. Ibid.

CHAPTER 12: "YOU DON'T SPEAK FOR ME, CINDY"

1. Cindy Sheehan, "Speak for Yourself," CommonDreams.org, February 25, 2006, www.commondreams.org/scriptfiles/views06/February2006.htm.

CHAPTER 15: SHEEHAN V. SHEEHAN

1. Cindy Sheehan, Interview with Chris Matthews, *Hardball,* August 16, 2005.

2. Cindy Sheehan, interview with Keith Olbermann, *Countdown with Keith Olbermann,* August 11, 2005.

3. Cindy Sheehan, *Not One More Mother's Child* (Kihei, HI: Koa Books, 2005), 99.

4. Darksyde, "Interview with Gold Star Mother Cindy Sheehan,"

August 1, 2005, http://darksyde.dailykos.com/storyonly/2005/8/1
/2161/52638.

CHAPTER 17: JUST US—NO PEACE

1. David Rolland, "American Patriot," *San Diego City Beat,* April 19,
2006.

2. Cindy Sheehan, "The Antiwar Movement?" *Palestine Chronicle,*
April 11, 2006.

CONCLUSION

1. Nathan Burchfiel, "I Have to Pay My Bills Too," CNSnews.com,
September 28, 2005, http://www.cnsnews.com/ViewPolitics.asp?Page
=%5CPolitics%5Carchive%5C200509%5CPOL20050928a.html.

INDEX